D1563558

"This is the devotional I didn't know I was missing. Dodge connects stories from Austen's life and the pages of her novels to her prayers and Scripture in fresh and insightful ways. An inspiring and illuminating look at the life and faith of a beloved author."

—Anne Bogel, author, *I'd Rather Be Reading: The Delights and Dilemmas of the Reading Life*

"*Praying with Jane* offers a fresh look at a familiar life. Ms. Dodge delivers a perfect blend of history and biography, revealing the true heart of Jane Austen through her handwritten prayers. Your own prayer life will be challenged and deepened as you daily study God's Word along with Jane."

—Laura Boyle, Austentation: Regency Accessories

"Practical, edifying, and informative, this guide will appeal to Janeites, scholars, and spiritual directors alike. Its pages are full of fascinating biographical details from Jane Austen's life interwoven with the powerful words of her prayers and the beauty, truth, and goodness of Scripture."

—Dr. Natasha Duquette, professor of English and author, *Veiled Intent: Dissenting Women's Aesthetic Approach to Biblical Interpretation*

"*Praying with Jane* is full of rich insights into the faith of one of our greatest English writers. It offers a window into her life and writings, as well as being a source of spiritual nourishment!"

—Terry Glaspey, author, *The Prayers of Jane Austen* and *75 Masterpieces Every Christian Should Know*

"In *Praying with Jane*, Dodge provides the reader with a way to examine the spiritual life of Jane Austen. The line-by-line encounter of each prayer makes Austen's prayers personal and relevant."

—Amanda Jacobs, composer/playwright and artist educator

"Rachel Dodge reminds us that the real Jane Austen prayed daily, attended services, and read the Bible and sermons for enlightenment and amendment of life. Excerpts from Austen's novels and letters are thoughtfully interwoven with Jane's own prayers and Dodge's meditations on the biblical texts Austen knew well in this inspiring month of devotions."

—Theresa M. Kenney, associate professor of English, University of Dallas

# PRAYING
*with*
# JANE

## 31 DAYS THROUGH THE PRAYERS OF JANE AUSTEN

## RACHEL DODGE

## BETHANYHOUSE
a division of Baker Publishing Group
Minneapolis, Minnesota

© 2018 by Rachel Dodge

Published by Bethany House Publishers
11400 Hampshire Avenue South
Bloomington, Minnesota 55438
www.bethanyhouse.com

Bethany House Publishers is a division of
Baker Publishing Group, Grand Rapids, Michigan

Printed in the United States of America

ISBN 978-0-7642-3215-2

Library of Congress Control Number: 2018940489

Unless otherwise indicated, Scripture quotations are from The Holy Bible, English Standard Version® (ESV®), copyright © 2001 by Crossway, a publishing ministry of Good News Publishers. Used by permission. All rights reserved. ESV Text Edition: 2011

Scripture quotations labeled KJV are from the King James Version of the Bible.

Scripture quotations labeled NASB are from the New American Standard Bible®, copyright © 1960, 1962, 1963, 1968, 1971, 1972, 1973, 1975, 1977, 1995 by The Lockman Foundation. Used by permission. (www.Lockman.org)

Scripture quotations labeled NIV are from the Holy Bible, New International Version®. NIV®. Copyright © 1973, 1978, 1984, 2011 by Biblica, Inc.™ Used by permission of Zondervan. All rights reserved worldwide. www.zondervan.com

Scripture quotations labeled NKJV are from the New King James Version®. Copyright © 1982 by Thomas Nelson, Inc. Used by permission. All rights reserved.

Scripture quotations labeled NLT are from the Holy Bible, New Living Translation, copyright © 1996, 2004, 2015 by Tyndale House Foundation. Used by permission of Tyndale House Publishers, Inc., Carol Stream, Illinois 60188. All rights reserved.

Jane Austen's novels are in the public domain. All quotations are taken from the R.W. Chapman scholarly edition: Austen, Jane. The Novels of Jane Austen. Edited by R. W. Chapman. 5 vols. 3rd ed. Oxford: Oxford University Press, 1988.

Jane Austen's prayers are in the public domain. All quotations are taken from the original manuscripts: Austen, Jane. "Prayers Composed by my ever dear sister." Manuscripts (two quarto sheets). The Elinor Raas Heller Rare Book Room, Mills College, Oakland, California.

Cover design by Rob Williams, InsideOutCreativeArts
Interior design by Jane Klein

Author is represented by Books & Such Literary Agency.

18   19   20   21   22   23   24        7   6   5   4   3   2   1

*To George and Ruth,*
who allowed me scope for the imagination;

*to Bobby,*
for giving me so much more than
diamond sunbursts and marble halls;

*and to Lizzy and Jack,*
who are the sweetest and the best.

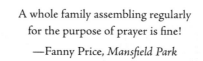

A whole family assembling regularly
for the purpose of prayer is fine!
—Fanny Price, *Mansfield Park*

# Contents

Introduction   9

## *Prayer One*

Day 1   Give Us Grace, Almighty Father   15

Day 2   An Ever-Present Help   19

Day 3   Fix Our Thoughts   23

Day 4   Give Us Pure Hearts   27

Day 5   A Day Well Spent   31

Day 6   Open Our Eyes   35

Day 7   Every Good and Perfect Gift   39

Day 8   Under His Care   43

Day 9   Help for the Helpless   47

Day 10   A Genuine Faith   51

## *Prayer Two*

Day 11   Look Down with Favor   57

Day 12   Make Us Mindful   61

Day 13   Invade Our Habits   65

Day 14   Guard Our Hearts   69

Day 15   A Good Father   73

Day 16   A Benevolent Spirit   77

Day 17   Give Us Patience   81
Day 18   Keep the Night Watches   85
Day 19   To the Farthest Reaches   89
Day 20   A Fervent Faith   93

*Prayer Three*

Day 21   Fervent in Prayer   99
Day 22   Redeeming the Time   103
Day 23   Make Us Like You   107
Day 24   Search Our Hearts, O God   111
Day 25   Inexpressible Joy   115
Day 26   Blessed Beyond Deserving   119
Day 27   Morning Dawns and Evening Fades   123
Day 28   Go into the World   127
Day 29   Look with Compassion   131
Day 30   Thy Heavenly Kingdom   135
Day 31   Our Father   139

Epilogue: A Lasting Legacy   143
Special Invitation   146
Acknowledgments   149
Notes   152
Bibliography   158
About the Author   160

# INTRODUCTION

Jane Austen is known for the beauty and romance of her words. As readers, we find ourselves engrossed in her characters and their lives, loves, and losses. Whole days and nights can pass as she transports us to another time and place filled with bows, curtsies, and drawing room dramas. And within the pages of her novels, we find enduring truths about life, love, family, and human nature. We become one with her characters and feel as though we know the woman who wrote them.

But Jane Austen was much more than a brilliant author. A devoted daughter, sister, aunt, and friend, she possessed intense feelings, strong opinions, and enduring faith. Besides her novels, she left us three beautiful prayers. Jane's sister, Cassandra, treasured these prayers, folded them together, and inscribed them with the words "Prayers Composed by my ever dear Sister Jane," to be kept safe for future generations.[1]

Jane's father, the Reverend George Austen, was an Anglican clergyman. According to family letters and documents, Reverend

Austen devoted himself to his work as a spiritual leader in his parish and his home. Thus, Jane grew up immersed in the traditions of the Church of England.

In her book *Jane Austen's Anglicanism*, Laura Mooneyham White describes what daily religious life looked like for the Austen family:

> What modern Christians cannot comprehend is the effect of liturgical repetition on the committed Anglican of Austen's day, who would have had family prayers for both Morning and Evening Prayer every day, two services of two to three hours each on Sunday, daily private prayers on awakening and on going to bed, and grace before each meal, with thanksgiving after.[2]

Part of Jane's religious upbringing was an intimate knowledge of the devotional literature of her day. In her book *The Parson's Daughter*, Irene Collins notes that Jane "cherished" William Vickers' *Companion to the Altar* and "made constant use of the prayers and meditations included in it."[3] She also most likely knew many of the prayers in the Book of Common Prayer by heart. It is no surprise, then, that Jane's prayers echo their language.

In the evening, Jane's family enjoyed reading out loud from novels, poetry, and sermons, as well as from the entertaining stories Jane wrote. Before going to bed, the family prayed and read the Bible together. In a letter she wrote to Cassandra, in reference to a Sunday evening in which they were unable to attend church, Jane writes, "In the evening we had the Psalms and Lessons, and a sermon at home."[4] It is possible that Jane shared her prayers during intimate evening devotions such as these.

Studying Jane's prayers, letters, and novels, walking the country lanes around her home, and sitting on the benches in her garden all give us a better sense of Jane's life and personality. By all accounts, she was a delight. Made up of equal parts sweetness and spice, faith and folly, she never took herself too seriously. She possessed an amazing intellect yet laughed easily. Her comments about herself and others in her letters sparkle with good-natured humor. She was funny and opinionated one moment, then concerned and compassionate the next.

Reading Jane's prayers is a bit like looking into her heart. In them, we get to know another side of Jane's personality—a more serious and reverent side. They reveal a genuine, practical faith in Jesus Christ. Every line displays a balance of robust belief and tender intimacy. And like her novels, Jane's prayers contain meaning that reaches far beyond eloquent words or graceful phrases. They are personal and reflective, passionate and thorough. Each one includes a time of thanksgiving, confession, petition, and intercession. They show us the value she placed on corporate and family prayer. Even more, Jane's prayers reveal her closeness to God and her desire to be more like Christ.

This book is designed to help you savor Jane's prayers, to understand each one more fully, and to delve into the treasure trove of biblical and practical applications found in each line. Though each of Jane's three prayers would have most likely been read to her family in its entirety, this book allows you to study them slowly and carefully. At the end of each day's devotional, you'll find an invitation to pray and a sample prayer. The sample prayers are meant as a starting point for your own extended time of prayer.

This book is broken down into three sections, one for each of Jane's prayers, with ten devotions per prayer. The capitalization and punctuation of her prayers have been reproduced as closely to the original manuscripts as possible. On Day 31, you'll find an examination of the last line of each prayer, each of which leads into the Lord's Prayer, as well as reflections on the Lord's Prayer itself. The original manuscripts only include the first few words of the Lord's Prayer and an ellipsis. Thus, the version of the Lord's Prayer used on Day 31 is taken from the 1662 *Book of Common Prayer*, the version Jane would most likely have known.

As you begin your exploration of Jane's prayers, take time to settle yourself into a quiet spot with a cup of tea or coffee and your journal. This is your invitation to know Jane better . . . and the God she loved. As you "pray with Jane," may the Lord unlock profound truths and hidden promises as you come near to him in expectation.

# ❧ *Prayer One* ❧

*G*ive us grace, Almighty Father, so to pray, as to deserve
to be heard, to address thee with our Hearts, as with our
Lips. Thou art every where present, from Thee no secret
can be hid; May the knowledge of this, teach us to fix our Thoughts
on Thee, with Reverence & Devotion that we pray not in vain.

Look with Mercy on the Sins we have this day committed, &
in Mercy make us feel them deeply, that our Repentance may be
sincere, and our Resolutions stedfast of endeavouring against the
commission of such in future. Teach us to understand the sinful-
ness of our own Hearts, and bring to our knowledge every fault
of Temper and every evil Habit in which we may have indulged to
the discomfort of our fellow-creatures, and the danger of our own
Souls. May we now, and on each return of night, consider how
the past day has been spent by us, what have been our prevailing Thoughts, Words and Actions during it, and how far we can
acquit ourselves of Evil. Have we thought irreverently of Thee,

13

have we disobeyed Thy Commandments, have we neglected any known Duty, or willingly given pain to any human Being? Incline us to ask our Hearts these questions Oh! God, and save us from deceiving ourselves by Pride or Vanity.

Give us a thankful sense of the Blessings in which we live, of the many comforts of our Lot; that we may not deserve to lose them by Discontent or Indifference.

Be Gracious to our Necessities, and guard us, and all we love, from Evil this night. May the sick and afflicted, be now, & ever thy care; and heartily do we pray for the safety of all that travel by Land or by Sea, for the comfort & protection of the Orphan & Widow, & that thy pity may be shewn, upon all Captives & Prisoners.

Above all other blessings Oh! God, for ourselves, & our fellow-creatures, we implore Thee to quicken our sense of thy Mercy in the redemption of the World, of the Value of that Holy Religion in which we have been brought up, that we may not, by our own Neglect, throw away the Salvation Thou hast given us, nor be Christians only in name. Hear us Almighty God, for His sake who has redeemed us, & taught us thus to pray.

Our Father which art in Heaven . . .

—Jane Austen

## *Day 1*

# GIVE US GRACE,
# ALMIGHTY FATHER

*Give us grace, Almighty Father, so to pray, as to deserve to be heard, to address thee with our Hearts, as with our Lips.*

Born in Steventon, Hampshire, on December 16, 1775, Jane Austen entered the world a full month later than her mother "expected."[1] Her entire family eagerly anticipated her arrival, and from the beginning, Jane enjoyed a close relationship with her father. After his death when Jane was nearly twenty, she wrote these words to her brother Frank: "His tenderness as a father, who can do justice to?"[2] She called him "an excellent Father" and referred to "the sweet, benevolent smile which always distinguished him."[3]

Jane's personal experience of a father surely shaped her understanding of God as a father. She grew up with a loving, attentive father—one who was interested, kind, and present. Jane begins this first prayer by asking for God's "grace" (or help) to pray. She desires to speak to him from her heart, not just with her lips, and refers to him as her "Almighty Father."

The name *Almighty Father* combines two of the most beautiful and contradictory forces in the universe: strength and love. The term *Almighty* refers to God's power to save us (Romans 1:16), protect us, and direct us. The word *Father* indicates a father-child relationship that comes by faith in Christ. Together, this name speaks of a father who is not only all-powerful but is also actively involved in every part of our lives.

Jane's father instilled in her a love for literature, gave her full access to his library, and encouraged her to use her writing talent from an early age. He most likely placed her first quill in her hand and taught her to write her letters.

As adopted sons and daughters in Christ, we also enjoy special father-child privileges and have full access to God as his children (Ephesians 2:18). We can come to him in prayer, anytime, anywhere.

> To all who did receive him, who believed in his name, he gave the right to become children of God.
>
> —John 1:12

Jane comes to her "Almighty Father," asking for the "grace . . . to pray," that she might "address" God with her heart and not only her lips. Her prayer echoes Matthew 15:8, in which Jesus says, "This people honors me with their lips, but their heart is far from me." Her prayer also reminds us that our prayers don't need to be elaborate or fancy because God "looks on the heart," not on the "outward appearance" (1 Samuel 16:7).

Just as Jane could go into her father's library for a book or to ask him a question, you can go to your Almighty Father—your strong father—for the help, advice, and love you crave. A strong father watches over his children, provides for their needs, and protects them from harm. He isn't impatient with their baby steps or irritated when they need help. The same is true of your Al-

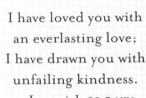

I have loved you with an everlasting love; I have drawn you with unfailing kindness.
—Jeremiah 31:3 NIV

mighty Father. God loves you, cares for you, and *delights* in you.

### Invitation to Pray

Are you in need of a loving, strong father in your life? When you pray, you call on the same Almighty God who, with his very breath, sent winds strong enough to split the Red Sea down the middle when the Israelites were trapped against it and needed a way of escape. Cry out to your Almighty Father today, right now, in your time of need. He alone possesses the power to bring order out of chaos, move mountains, and split seas.

Take this time to pray on your own, tucked away in a quiet place where you can be open and vulnerable. Pray from your heart and ask God to lead you as you pray. Invite him into your day, your week, your joys, and your troubles. He has the power, the desire, *and* the ability to help.

### Let Us Pray

*Thank you, God, for being my Father. Thank you for sending Jesus to die for me so I could become your child. Help me to draw close to you now and talk to you like a child to her father. I open my heart to you and ask for your grace to pray. Please help me to understand how strong you are and how much you love me. I want to know you more. I need your strength and help in this area of my life: [your specific needs]. In Jesus' name, Amen.*

But from there you will seek the Lord your God and you will find him, if you search after him with all your heart and with all your soul.
—Deuteronomy 4:29

### Special Invitation

If you wish to ask Jesus to be your Savior, you'll find a Special Invitation section at the end of this devotional on page 146 that's just for you. There, you can learn about how to become a child of God.

# *Day 2*

## AN EVER-PRESENT HELP

*Thou art every where present, from Thee no secret can be hid . . .*

Whether Jane was born, her father wrote: "We have now another girl, a present plaything for her sister Cassy, and a future companion."[1] His words proved prophetic indeed. Jane's only sister in a rather large family, Cassandra was, from the very first, Jane's closest earthly companion. In fact, when Cassandra was old enough to go to school, little Jane went with her, not because she was old enough, but "because she would have been miserable without her sister."[2] Throughout her life, Jane cherished Cassandra's friendship, and the two sisters were rarely apart.

In this line of her prayer, Jane focuses on God's nearness. Her words remind us that the Lord, even more than any earthly friend or companion, is always with us. Her prayer points us to the promise that we are never alone. It brings to mind the picture of a best friend—one who is always there, knows all our secrets, and will come whenever we call. In Proverbs, we read that "there are 'friends' who destroy each other, but a real friend sticks closer than a brother" (18:24 NLT). That friend is Jesus, who gave his life as a ransom for yours, so you could be set free from sin and death and enjoy a relationship with God.

This line of Jane's prayer speaks of God's watchful presence over his children, for their good and for their protection. Her words "Thou art every where present" are intimate and tender; they evoke the image of a bird in a nest, comfortable and warm. The winds and the rains come, but the bird is happy and safe. In the same way, our lives rest in the palm of God's hand. He is all around us, even in the very air we breathe. God's unbroken presence equals peace and security.

> I will never leave you
> nor forsake you.
> —Hebrews 13:5

When Jane was young, her mother once observed that "if Cassandra were going to have her head cut off, Jane would insist on sharing her fate."[3] As adults, Jane and Cassandra were always together, walking, talking, and sharing confidences. When they were apart, they wrote long, newsy letters, sharing the minute details of their everyday lives. In Jane's letters, she addressed her sister as "My dearest Cassandra." The two enjoyed a close relationship through those letters, even when they were separated by weeks and miles.

There is comfort in knowing that nothing is hidden from the people we love most. With our most cherished friends or family members, we share almost everything. The same is true in our relationship with God. Jane says no secret "can be hid" from God. This speaks of the intimacy we have with God. He knows our hearts fully, even more than a close friend or family member. We need not fear God's complete knowledge of us; for the child of God, this is a comfort. We don't think a thought, feel a feeling, or say a word that surprises him. He knows us through and through.

O Lord, you have searched me and known me!
You know when I sit down and when I rise up; you discern my thoughts from afar. You search out my path and my lying down and are acquainted with all my ways. Even before a word is on my tongue, behold, O Lord, you know it altogether.
—Psalm 139:1–4

### Invitation to Pray

Do you need God's presence right now? Do you feel alone? Jane's prayer invites you to personally know Jesus, who is the one who is "closer than a brother." When storms of trouble, confusion, illness, or sorrow hit our lives, it's common to feel alone. Jane's prayer reminds us that God is always near. You can stop right now and talk to him; he's right next to you.

Or perhaps you long for a "dearest Cassandra" in your life. Let today's reading encourage you to reach out to another Christian for friendship. If you're not sure where to start, you might consider joining a Bible study or prayer group at your church.

### Let Us Pray

*Heavenly Father, thank you for the promise that you are always near to me. I'm glad you're not a God who is far off. Please help me now to talk to you as I do to my best friend. I want to tell you everything and draw close to you. I don't want to keep any secrets from you. Thank you that you promise to never leave me or forsake me. I feel alone in this area of my life: [your specific needs]. In Jesus' name, Amen.*

God is our refuge and strength,
an ever-present help in trouble.
—Psalm 46:1 NIV

# *Day 3*

## FIX OUR THOUGHTS

*May the knowledge of this, teach us to fix our Thoughts on Thee, with Reverence & Devotion that we pray not in vain.*

When Captain Wentworth writes to Anne at the end of *Persuasion*, he says: "For you alone, I think and plan."[1] Anne stands at a window talking with another gentleman, "not very near,"[2] and yet Wentworth can think of nothing but her and the distinct sound of her voice. We later read that Anne's eyes "devoured" the words in his letter.[3] In perhaps the most romantic scene in all of English literature, we see two people with their eyes and thoughts completely *fixed* on each other.

Jane paints a similar picture of whole-hearted devotion to God in this portion of her prayer: She prays for the "knowledge" of God's continual presence to teach her to "fix [her] Thoughts" on him. Like anyone who has ever sat down to pray, Jane evidently understood how easy it is to become distracted. She desired,

23

therefore, to pray with "Reverence & Devotion." Jane's words also suggest that she wanted God on the throne of her heart and at the center of her vision.

We often assume Jane lived a simple life with no worries or distractions in her small village in the English countryside. However, with wars abroad, two brothers in the navy, times of illness (before antibiotics or ambulances), and deaths in the family, Jane surely experienced her own set of woes. She also spent a great deal of time traveling to visit neighbors and friends both near and far. And, in the midst of it all, she wrote and rewrote her novels. When Jane came to pray in the evening, she often undoubtedly needed refreshment and refocus.

You shall love the Lord your God with all your heart and with all your soul and with all your strength and with all your mind.
—Luke 10:27

Jane's prayer is a wonderful reminder to fix our thoughts on God in prayer and throughout the day. Her words echo the many verses in the Bible that speak of the fruit that comes from keeping our thoughts focused on God. Giving him our full attention not only brings him honor, it also has many benefits. When we look to God alone, we find everything we need.

As we set our minds on "things that are above, not on things that are on earth" (Colossians 3:2), we turn our eyes from our earthly problems and look heavenward. We find refreshment and regain an eternal perspective. When we focus on God's character and attributes, his strength and nearness shrink our problems to the appropriate size. As the psalmist says, "I lift up my eyes to the mountains—where does my help come from? My help comes from the Lord, the Maker of heaven and earth" (Psalm 121:1–2 NIV).

> I keep my eyes always on the Lord. With him at my right hand, I will not be shaken.
> —Psalm 16:8 NIV

Fixing our eyes on God is also an antidote for anxiousness. In Philippians 4, we read that "the Lord is at hand" (v. 5). Paul says, "do not be anxious about anything, but in everything by prayer and supplication with thanksgiving let your requests be made known to God" (v. 6). As a result, "the peace of God, which surpasses all understanding, will guard your hearts and your minds in Christ Jesus" (v. 7). The practice of centering our thoughts on God brings peace.

## Invitation to Pray

Jane's desire to "fix" her eyes on God is a great inspiration for us. Most of us have a lot on our minds each day. We have a constant list of to-dos running through our heads. When difficulties arise, it's easy to focus more on the issues at hand than on God. Do you have a heavy burden? A nagging fear? Take this time now to lay everything before the Lord in prayer and ask him to help you focus your eyes on him.

If you sometimes feel distracted when you pray, try writing your prayers in a journal or praying out loud as Jane and her family did. Praying with others, singing praise songs, and memorizing Scripture can all help you become more enthralled with the glory of who Jesus is. These practices help keep your eyes on *Christ*, not the *crisis*.

### Let Us Pray

*Heavenly Father, thank you for reminding me to look to you throughout the day. Help me to know you better and to pray with reverence and devotion. I want to be captivated by you. Please stir my affections for you, Lord! The things I'm most concerned about and distracted by today are: [your specific needs]. I ask you to give me the mind of Christ and show me a Bible verse to write out for today. In Jesus' name, Amen.*

You will keep in perfect peace all who trust in you, all whose thoughts are fixed on you!
—Isaiah 26:3 NLT

# *Day 4*

## GIVE US PURE HEARTS

—⟪⟪◆⟫⟫—

*Look with Mercy on the Sins we have this day committed, & in Mercy make us feel them deeply, that our Repentance may be sincere, and our Resolutions stedfast of endeavouring against the commission of such in future. Teach us to understand the sinful-ness of our own Hearts, and bring to our knowledge every fault of Temper and every evil Habit in which we may have indulged to the discomfort of our fellow-creatures, and the danger of our own Souls.*

When we think of a Jane Austen heroine in need of sincere repentance, Emma Woodhouse comes to mind. When Emma speaks cruelly to Miss Bates and says she's dull in front of everyone at Box Hill, we cringe with pain and agony. Austen tells us that in Emma's moment of irritation, she "could not resist."[1] She opens her mouth and lets it rip.

Mr. Knightley tells Emma later that it "was badly done . . . in thoughtless spirits, and the pride of the moment, [to] laugh at her" and "humble her."[2] In response, Emma feels "anger against herself, mortification, and deep concern."[3] On the ride home, she is "most forcibly struck. The truth of this representation there was no denying. She felt it at her heart. How could she have been so brutal, so cruel to Miss Bates!"[4] Emma spends the evening in serious reflection and visits Miss Bates the next morning to make amends as best she can.

In this portion of her prayer, Jane moves into a time of reflection and confession. She asks God to help her "feel" her sins deeply, in order to bring about a "sincere" repentance. She wants to take an honest look at her heart, temper, and habits. Her stirring words remind us that even the smallest roots of discontentment, jealousy, lust, bitterness, or anger can quickly grow if left unattended.

When Emma speaks harshly to Miss Bates, it isn't the first time she's felt tempted to say something mean. She's already said hurtful, disdainful things about Miss Bates in her heart many times. She's rehearsed and polished those words until they sit poised and ready on the tip of her tongue—sharp, stinging, and perfectly aimed to hit their mark.

> For out of the abundance of the heart the mouth speaks.
> —Matthew 12:34 NKJV

The same thing happens to us when we feel annoyed or irritated by someone, especially when we let those feelings build over time. In Jane's prayer, she asks God to "look with Mercy" on their sins and to "teach [them] to understand the sinfulness of [their] Hearts," "every fault of Temper," and "every evil Habit" that causes discomfort to others. This points to the biblical concept of guarding our hearts and thoughts: "Keep your heart with all vigilance, for from it flow the springs of life" (Proverbs 4:23).

Eventually, if we're not careful, everything we think or feel makes its way out of our mouths.

We've all had a Box Hill moment, when we said or did something we later regretted. When we slip up, we tend to bear down and try harder, but our own limited supply of natural goodness, kindness, and gentleness can only

My grace is sufficient
for you, for my power
is made perfect
in weakness.

—2 Corinthians 12:9 NIV

carry us so far. Instead, we need to turn to Jesus, repent of our sins, and take hold of the "incredible greatness of God's power for us," the very same "mighty power that raised Christ from the dead" (Ephesians 1:19–20 NLT).

### Invitation to Pray

Do you wish you could erase and re-record certain moments in your life when you said or did the wrong thing? We all do. It's important in those moments to humble ourselves, ask forgiveness of the person we hurt or offended, and come to God in prayer, asking for a change of heart. When we repent, we stop following our own selfish nature, turn around, and walk toward God.

Take this time now to experience the blessed relief of repentance. When you turn and run into God's arms, you find profound peace. So often we picture an angry or disappointed God, but he is waiting for you to come. Acts 3:19 says that when we repent, "the times of refreshing shall come from the presence of the Lord" (KJV).

### Let Us Pray

*Thank you, Lord, for your faithfulness and your strength. Please show me the areas of my heart, temper, and habits that you want to refine. As the psalmist prayed, please "set a guard, O Lord, over my mouth; keep watch over the door of my lips!" (Psalm 141:3). I confess to you now my negative thoughts regarding: [your specific confession]. Make my heart clean and new again. I turn to you now for refreshment and revival. In Jesus' name, Amen.*

Create in me a clean heart,
O God, and renew a right spirit within me.
—Psalm 51:10

# *Day 5*

## A DAY WELL SPENT

*May we now, and on each return of night, consider how the past day has been spent by us, what have been our prevailing Thoughts, Words and Actions during it, and how far we can acquit ourselves of Evil.*

J ane's niece, Marianne Knight, once shared a charming peek into a visit with Jane when she was young: Marianne said her aunt Jane would "sit quietly working beside the fire in the library, saying nothing for a good while, and then would suddenly burst out laughing, jump up and run across the room to a table where pens and paper were lying, write something down, and then come back to the fire and go on quietly working as before."[1]

From this description, we see that while Jane sat and worked (needlework) quietly, lines, descriptions, and plot ideas for her novels came to her in delightful bursts. And it's clear that she found her stories and characters just as amusing as we do! But this picture of Jane shows us something else: She had a rich inner life. She went about her daily tasks with a happy spirit. In fact, it was *while* she sat with her family and sewed that she sometimes found inspiration!

In this portion of her prayer, Jane considers "how the past day has been spent." Since she spent her days writing, gardening, walking, and working, it's hard to imagine that she had much need to "acquit" herself of evil. So why did Jane want to think back on her day so carefully? Why was she concerned about her "prevailing Thoughts, Words and Actions"? Simply put, Jane wanted to spend her days well.

One thing have I asked of the Lord, that will I seek after: that I may dwell in the house of the Lord all the days of my life, to gaze upon the beauty of the Lord and to inquire in his temple.

—Psalm 27:4

Marianne's description could have been totally different. Jane could have just as easily snapped at her young niece for making noise, told everyone she had a writing deadline, and slammed the door. She could have declared needlework a boring, repetitive task and herself too intelligent for such menial jobs. Instead, she appears to have spent the time in happy reflection. And at the end of the day, Jane and her family set aside their work for a time of prayer.

Many things vie for our attention each day, and our personal definition of a day well spent might mean a variety of things.

Thankfully, Jesus simplifies this question for us in Luke 10. When sisters Mary and Martha welcome Jesus into their home for a meal, Martha becomes overly "distracted with much serving." Her sister Mary, however, "sat at the Lord's feet and listened to his teaching" (Luke 10:39–40). When Martha speaks to Jesus about her problem, he gently shows her there's only "one thing" truly necessary: time spent with him.

But the Lord answered her, "Martha, Martha, you are anxious and troubled about many things, but one thing is necessary. Mary has chosen the good portion, which will not be taken away from her."
—Luke 10:41–42

Jane's prayer echoes these verses and points us to a wonderful end-of-day habit she made of reflecting back on her day. When we take time to "consider how the past day has been spent," it allows us to think carefully about how we spend our days.

## Invitation to Pray

Considering your days, what is the prevailing focus of your thoughts, words, and actions? What consumes you? Mary chose the "good portion" of her day—the part that will last forever. The *one thing* we take with us throughout our lives and into eternity is our relationship with Jesus. Whether we find ourselves married or single, in good times or bad, close to home or across the world, Jesus is our constant.

Jesus calls out to you today with the kind words, "Martha, Martha." Can you hear him? His voice is soft and gentle. He invites you to set everything down and come sit with him. We often feel "anxious and troubled about many things," but when we spend time with Jesus, everything else falls into place.

### Let Us Pray

*Thank you, Lord, for reminding me that a day well spent is a day spent with you. Please give me the self-control to put down my work and spend time with you each day. I need time at your feet more than I need anything else. I find it hard to stop to read my Bible and pray because: [your specific needs]. Please build in me a deep yearning for more of you. I invite you now into every part of my day. In Jesus' name, Amen.*

But Jesus Himself would often
slip away to the wilderness and pray.
—Luke 5:16 NASB

# *Day 6*

## OPEN OUR EYES

*Have we thought irreverently of Thee, have we disobeyed Thy
Commandments, have we neglected any known Duty, or willingly
given pain to any human Being? Incline us to ask our Hearts
these questions Oh! God, and save us from deceiving ourselves
by Pride or Vanity.*

When Elizabeth Bennet reads Mr. Darcy's letter of expla-
nation in *Pride and Prejudice*, she is ashamed of her own
pride and vanity: "'How despicably I have acted!' she [cries]; 'I,
who have prided myself on my discernment! I, who have valued
myself on my abilities! . . . Had I been in love, I could not have
been more wretchedly blind! But vanity, not love, has been my
folly.' She ends with this: "Till this moment I never knew myself."[1]

Elizabeth Bennet feels especially humiliated by her misjudg-
ment of Mr. Wickham. She, who prides herself on her ability to
judge well, fails to discern his true character. She judges him by

his outer appearance and his "person, countenance, air, and walk."[2] She is charmed by his "agreeable manner" and is a "happy woman" when he sits with her, after catching the attention of "almost every female eye."[3] Ultimately, Elizabeth's own pride deceives her.

In this portion of her prayer, Jane prays for the ability to see herself clearly, citing "Pride or Vanity" as common causes of spiritual self-deception. She asks God to "incline" her to ask difficult questions of her own heart. She asks God to show her if she's "thought irreverently" of him," "disobeyed [his] Commandments," "neglected any known Duty," or "willingly given pain to any human Being."

The Bible has plenty to say about pride. In 2 Chronicles 26, King Uzziah becomes king when he is only sixteen years old. His reign starts off well: "And he did what was right in the eyes of the Lord, according to all that his father Amaziah had done. He set himself to seek God in the days of Zechariah, who instructed him in the fear of God, and as long as he sought the Lord, God made him prosper" (vv. 4–5). Uzziah experiences victory in battle, builds tall towers, gains great wealth, and experiences fame (vv. 6–15). That's when it all falls apart: "But when he was strong, he grew proud, to his destruction. For he was unfaithful to the Lord his God and entered the temple of the Lord to burn incense on the altar of incense" (v. 16).

> Let anyone who thinks that he stands take heed lest he fall.
> —1 Corinthians 10:12

Jane's prayer points to an inescapable truth: Pride and vanity lead us astray because they cause blindness. It happened in the Garden of Eden; it happens daily to each of us. Uzziah's pride in his own abilities and accomplishments caused his downfall. He began to think of the victories as his, the wealth as his, and the success as his. He forgot God.

Jane's prayer reminds us to continually ask God to show us our true selves. When we start to think too highly of ourselves, we inevitably lose our footing and trip. It's important to look to the solidity of God's perspective—not our own self-centered reflections—when we come to him in prayer. Like Jane, we can ask God to open our eyes and help us ask our own hearts these difficult questions, so that we aren't deceived.

> Pride goes before destruction, and a haughty spirit before a fall.
> —Proverbs 16:18

### Invitation to Pray

What is the state of your heart today? How do you see yourself? Most of us don't set out to willfully disobey God, break his commandments, neglect our duties, or hurt others, yet we do all of those things all too often. And unfortunately, our own pride can blind us to our biggest weaknesses.

When you pray, start by asking God to give you a spiritual vision check, so you can have a right view of yourself. Spending time with God is the best way to find our spiritual true north. It's also important to read God's Word regularly and systematically, so that you can look objectively at your life through the lens of Scripture and align yourself with it.

### Let Us Pray

*Lord, thank you for the reminder that I need a vision check when it comes to pride and vanity. Please show me what you see so I can pray with an open, honest heart. I want to be more like you, transformed by the renewing of my mind as I read my Bible and pray. Please form in me a humble heart. I need your perspective in this area of my life: [your specific needs]. In Jesus' name, Amen.*

Do not be conformed to this world,
but be transformed by the renewal of your
mind, that by testing you may discern
what is the will of God, what is good
and acceptable and perfect.
—Romans 12:2

# Day 7

## EVERY GOOD AND PERFECT GIFT

*Give us a thankful sense of the Blessings in which we live, of the
many comforts of our Lot; that we may not deserve to lose them
by Discontent or Indifference.*

Jane was surrounded by the beauty of Hampshire's lush green
countryside for most of her life. In his book *Memoir of Jane
Austen*, James Edward Austen-Leigh ( Jane's nephew) describes
the idyllic paths, hedgerows, fields, and scenery Jane knew at Steventon, her home for the first 25 years of her life: "This was the
cradle of her genius. These were the first objects which inspired
her young heart with a sense of the beauties of nature. In strolls
along those wood-walks, thick-coming fancies rose in her mind,
and gradually assumed the forms in which they came forth to
the world."[1]

As an adult, Jane traveled to visit friends and family, spent time at her brother Edward Austen Knight's Godmersham estate in Kent, and lived with her family in Bath for a brief period. Several years after Reverend Austen passed away, Mrs. Austen, Cassandra, and Jane returned to the quiet Hampshire countryside when Edward offered them a small house, rent-free, on his scenic Chawton estate. Though Jane surely had her own share of troubles and sorrows, her everyday life was filled with family, friends, books, visiting, and church.

In this portion of her prayer, Jane asks God for "a thankful sense of the Blessings" and "comforts" in her life. Quite evidently, Jane had much for which to be thankful.

Thus, the last few words of this line reveal an important truth: Discontentment and indifference are two prime enemies of thankfulness.

> And the whole congregation of the people of Israel grumbled against Moses and Aaron in the wilderness.
> —Exodus 16:2

Discontentment is wishing things were different. It's common when we face trials, compare our lives to the lives of others, or start to think what we have isn't enough. Indifference is the state of being unmoved by the blessings that surround us. It's common during times of peace and abundance. Discontentment and indifference are both founded in a lack of thankfulness because when we grumble about our "lot," we're really grumbling against God.

Conversely, the apostle Paul says in his letter to the Philippians that he's learned the secret to contentment. Though he's been beaten, imprisoned, deserted, and shipwrecked, he says, "I know what it is to be in need, and I know what it is to have plenty. I have learned the secret of being content in any and every situation, whether well fed or hungry, whether living in plenty or in want" (Philippians 4:12 NIV). How did Paul *learn* this secret? First, by practice. Second, by praying with thanksgiving. In Philippians 4:6, he says, "Do not be anxious about anything, but in every situation, by prayer and petition, *with thanksgiving*, present your requests to God" (NIV, emphasis mine).

> I will bless the Lord at all times; his praise shall continually be in my mouth.
> —Psalm 34:1

Jane's prayer reminds us to make thanksgiving an integral part of our prayer lives as a powerful antidote against discontentment and indifference. When you fill your mouth with praise, it has less room for grumbling. Thanking God for what he has done and has promised to do shifts your focus from what you don't have to what you do.

### Invitation to Pray

Is there any area of your life where you detect discontentment or indifference? Do you sometimes forget thanksgiving? It takes silence and solitude to gain a "thankful sense" of the blessings in our lives. To truly experience the benefits of thanksgiving, we must slow down and meditate on God's goodness, faithfulness, and promises.

One way to stir up thankfulness is to thank God for all you have in Christ: You have new birth, a living hope, an inheritance kept in heaven, and the eternal gift of salvation (1 Peter 1:3–5). You can also look back on God's history of faithfulness toward the people in the Bible and in your own life. Take this time to stop and thank God for all of his blessings and confess any discontentment or indifference.

### Let Us Pray

*Almighty Father, thank you for the many blessings you've given me and the comforts you've provided. Thank you that you are faithful, that you have a plan for my life, and that I get to spend eternity with you. Jesus, you are the same yesterday, today, and forever. Please guard my heart against discontentment or indifference in this area of my life: [your specific needs]. In Jesus' name, Amen.*

Every good gift and every perfect gift is
from above, coming down from the Father
of lights, with whom there is no variation
or shadow due to change.
—James 1:17

## *Day 8*

# UNDER HIS CARE

*Be Gracious to our Necessities, and guard us, and all we love, from Evil this night. May the sick and afflicted, be now, & ever thy care . . .*

A fter thanking God for the many blessings in our lives, it's natural to then pray for God's continued provision, protection, and help. During Jane's lifetime, medical knowledge was still limited, people lived in remote homes and villages, ships sank, mothers died in childbirth, and wars claimed fathers and sons. Thus, Jane asks God to "be Gracious" toward their needs and "guard" them during the night. She also asks God to care for and watch over the "sick and afflicted."

When Marianne falls ill in *Sense and Sensibility*, Elinor spends her days "attending and nursing her"[1] and "carefully administering the cordials prescribed."[2] When, on the third evening, Marianne worsens, Elinor notices the change and resolves to sit with

Marianne through the night: "Mrs. Jennings, knowing nothing of any change in the patient, went unusually early to bed; her maid, who was one of the principal nurses, was recreating herself in the housekeeper's room, and Elinor remained alone with Marianne."[3]

This example of sisterly love is a picture of the type of care Jane prays about in this portion of her prayer. Here, she prays for God's protection and help for those in need, asking that those who are sick or afflicted would "be now, & ever [God's] care." She asks God to be *with* them in the difficulties and trials of life.

Jane's prayer echoes God's promise to never leave us or forsake us (Hebrews 13:5). In fact, Isaiah 49:16 says he has "engraved" the names of his people "on the palms of [his] hands." Being *with* God in our troubles—and knowing that he is *with* us in them—is one of the many benefits of an intimate relationship with Christ. The very name Immanuel means "God with us" (Matthew 1:23).

And behold,
I am with you always,
to the end of the age.
—Matthew 28:20

Even once Marianne begins to improve, Elinor stays by her side, "with little intermission ... calming every fear, satisfying every inquiry of her enfeebled spirits, supplying every succour, and watching almost every look and every breath."[4] Throughout Marianne's illness, Elinor watches her every day, every hour, looking for signs of hope, calling for the doctor, and finally sending Colonel Brandon to bring Mrs. Dashwood. It is only when Elinor is absolutely sure that Marianne is recovering that she "silence[s] every doubt."[5]

Elinor's care for Marianne helps explain what Jane means when she asks God to keep those who are afflicted in his care. First Corinthians 1:9 says that God calls believers "into the fellowship of his Son, Jesus Christ our Lord." The term *fellowship* means to be together, but it's more than just standing near someone; it means "partnership" or "participation."[6] This is the picture of Christ in our trials. He is not just next to us; he enters into and joins in our suffering.

Two are better than one, because they have a good reward for their toil. For if they fall, one will lift up his fellow. But woe to him who is alone when he falls and has not another to lift him up!
—Ecclesiastes 4:9–10

### Invitation to Pray

Are you sick, afflicted, in trouble, or alone? Often, our prayers center on the alleviation of pain and suffering in times of trial, but Jane's prayer reminds us to also pray for God's presence *in* our suffering. If you're going through a difficult time, you can pray for God to encourage, comfort, and strengthen you.

Or perhaps you know someone who is ill or suffering. Take this time to lift him or her up in prayer and ask God to show you how to help. You can take a meal, visit the hospital, hold a hand, make a phone call, or write a note as a tangible expression of God's love. When you reach out to those who are suffering, you remind them of God's care for them.

### Let Us Pray

*Jesus, thank you for being with me every day and every night. Please open my eyes today to see the specific ways you are at work in my life. I ask for your comfort and protection today. I lift up to you my concerns and afflictions: [your specific needs]. I also want to bring before you those I love who are in need of your comfort and presence: [their names and needs]. In Jesus' name, Amen.*

I have said these things to you, that in me
you may have peace. In the world you will
have tribulation. But take heart;
I have overcome the world.
—John 16:33

# *Day 9*

## HELP FOR THE HELPLESS

*. . . and heartily do we pray for the safety of all that travel by Land or by Sea, for the comfort & protection of the Orphan & Widow, & that thy pity may be shewn, upon all Captives & Prisoners.*

This line in Jane's prayer reminds us that we are God's hands and feet here on earth. It specifically echoes the biblical passages that teach us to care for orphans and widows ( James 1:27) and visit prisoners (Hebrews 13:3). During Jesus' earthly ministry, he fed, taught, healed, and cared for the people around him. As his followers, we are extensions of him, called to help the helpless and defend the powerless.

In Jane's novels, we see many examples of practical caretaking. Mr. Knightley gives baskets of apples to the Bateses and sends his carriage for them. Edward Ferrars's father sets up an annuity in his will for three elderly servants. Mr. Darcy uses his power and

47

wealth to save Lydia from ruin. And Sir John Middleton offers Barton Cottage to Mrs. Dashwood "on very easy terms" after her husband's death.[1]

Jane's own mother, Mrs. Austen, survived Reverend Austen by nearly 22 years. Her son Edward provided a home for her, Cassandra, and Jane. Mrs. Austen once wrote to her sister-in-law Mrs. Leigh Perrot about her financial status as a widow, saying, "[Edward] is most kind and liberal: he allows me £200 a year, gives me my house rent, supplies me plentifully with wood and makes me many presents—and often asks Cassandra if she is sure I have enough, as if not he would most willingly give me more . . ."[2]

Religion that is pure and undefiled before God the Father is this: to visit orphans and widows in their affliction, and to keep oneself unstained from the world.

—James 1:27

Jane prays "heartily" here for God's comfort and protection over widows and orphans and for God's pity on captives and prisoners. When we pray heartily for others, we come closer to the heart of God, "father to the fatherless, defender of widows," the one who "sets the prisoners free" (Psalm 68:5–6 NLT).

When we remember that we were once spiritual orphans, but that God sent his son to die for us so that we might become his sons and daughters, God's desire to win souls, heal brokenness, and rescue hearts becomes our desire.

Jane's prayer gets right to the heart of what Jesus did when he was here on earth. He healed bodies and filled bellies; even more, he gave people spiritual food and drink (John 4:14). As his followers, our Christian faith is marked by our care for the weak and powerless and our willingness to help them physically and spiritually.

Jane's prayer reminds us that though we cannot comfort every widow, orphan, and prisoner, we can reach out to one lonely man, woman, or child with the love of Christ. And no matter our age, health, or financial circumstances, we can pray for those in need.

> For I was hungry and you gave me food, I was thirsty and you gave me drink, I was a stranger and you welcomed me, I was naked and you clothed me, I was sick and you visited me, I was in prison and you came to me.
> —Matthew 25:35–36

### Invitation to Pray

Do you know someone who needs to experience the tangible love of God in their lives? Some people can't fathom God's love because no one has ever shown them real, giving, sacrificial love. Perhaps the Lord is calling you to practically care for orphans, widows, or prisoners. Or maybe he's calling you to support people who are serving on the front lines in these areas.

Sometimes orphans and widows, captives and prisoners come in different shapes and sizes. Many people feel trapped in their circumstances or imprisoned by health issues. Many children, teenagers, and young adults need a spiritual parent. Take this time now to pray *heartily* for the person you know who needs a practical and spiritual touch from the Lord.

### Let Us Pray

*Heavenly Father, thank you for reminding me that I have a special job to do. Please give me the mind of Christ and show me someone for whom I can pray. If you had my hands, my feet, and my mouth, what would you do today? I confess that I get caught up in my own life and don't always take the time to look around me. Please show me how to reach out to others in need: [specific names]. In Jesus' name, Amen.*

Give, and it will be given to you.
A good measure, pressed down, shaken
together and running over, will be poured
into your lap. For with the measure you use,
it will be measured to you.
—Luke 6:38 NIV

## *Day 10*

# A GENUINE FAITH

*Above all other blessings Oh! God, for ourselves, & our fellow–*
*creatures, we implore Thee to quicken our sense of thy Mercy in*
*the redemption of the World, of the Value of that Holy Religion*
*in which we have been brought up, that we may not, by our own*
*Neglect, throw away the Salvation Thou hast given us, nor be*
*Christians only in name.*

This line in Jane's prayer is passionate and sobering. It's a warning against spiritual drowsiness and a reminder to be alert and awake in our faith. Jane "implores" God to "quicken" her sense of the "Value of that Holy Religion in which" she was brought up, that she would not neglect her faith or be a Christian "only in name."

A prime example of false Christianity in Jane's novels is Mrs. Norris in *Mansfield Park*. Though she is a clergyman's wife, she exhibits character traits that are far from the heart of Christ. She claims she's "always ready enough to do for the good" of those she loves, but she only loves money and those who have it. She says, "I should hate myself if I were capable of neglecting [Fanny]," even though she mistreats and belittles Fanny continually. She also declares she "would rather deny [herself] the necessaries of life, than do an ungenerous thing," when in reality she is selfish and cares only for her own comfort.[1]

> These people come near to me with their mouth and honor me with their lips, but their hearts are far from me. Their worship of me is based on merely human rules they have been taught.
> —Isaiah 29:13 NIV

Many people identify as Christians "only in name" and do not value the "Holy Religion in which [they] have been brought up." They go through the motions of religion outwardly but are unchanged within. Others claim faith in God yet are consumed by habitual sin, selfish greed, pride, or lust. Some even use religion for personal gain, power, or rank.

Jesus said religious hypocrites are like "whitewashed tombs, which outwardly appear beautiful, but within are full of dead people's bones and all uncleanness" (Matthew 23:27). He said, "Beware of the scribes, who like to walk around in long robes, and love greetings in the marketplaces and the best seats in the synagogues and the places of honor at feasts, who devour widows' houses and for a pretense make long prayers" (Luke 20:46–47).

Conversely, Jesus describes genuine faith like this: "By this all people will know that you are my disciples, if you have love for one another" (John 13:35). The apostle John says believers ought to "walk in the same way in which [Jesus] walked" (1 John 2:6), meaning we begin to think, talk, and act more like Jesus as we grow in our faith. James 1:22 exhorts believers to "be doers of the word, and not hearers only," not just agreeing with the Bible but putting it into practice.

Jane also asks God to "quicken" her sense of God's "Mercy in the redemption of the World," which reminds us to pray for the salvation of others. As those who have been redeemed by the precious blood of Jesus, genuine believers value that "Holy Religion" more than anything else and desire to see others come to faith as well.

### Invitation to Pray

Do you want to live a life of genuine faith? Have you identified as a Christian "in name" but want to know

Therefore be imitators of God, as beloved children. And walk in love, as Christ loved us and gave himself up for us, a fragrant offering and sacrifice to God.
—Ephesians 5:1–2

Jesus as your personal Savior? Jane's prayer reminds us that true faith is not a set of rules or regulations, traditions or recitations; it's a living, breathing relationship with God that comes through faith in Christ.

Take this time now to consider what you believe. If you're a Christian and notice that some areas of your life don't line up with Scripture, take this time to pray over those issues. If you want to ask Jesus into your heart and begin a life of genuine faith, you can read about how to do that in the Special Invitation section at the back of this book on page 146.

### Let Us Pray

*Dearest Jesus, thank you for dying on the cross for my sins. Thank you for laying down your life so that I might live. Please help me now to walk as you walked. I want to love as you loved, give as you gave, and teach as you taught. Open my eyes to see where my walk doesn't match my talk. Please help me to live as a Christian, even behind closed doors, in this difficult area: [your specific needs]. In Jesus' name, Amen.*

Therefore if anyone is in Christ,
he is a new creature; the old things passed
away; behold, new things have come.
—2 Corinthians 5:17 NASB

# ❧ *Prayer Two* ❧

lmighty God! Look down with Mercy on thy Servants here assembled & accept the petitions now offered up unto thee.

*Pardon Oh God! the offences of the past day. We are conscious of many frailties; we remember with shame & contrition, many evil Thoughts & neglected duties, & we have perhaps sinned against Thee & against our fellow–creatures in many instances of which we have now no remembrance. Pardon Oh God! whatever thou hast seen amiss in us, & give us a stronger desire of resisting every evil inclination & weakening every habit of sin. Thou knowest the infirmity of our Nature, & the temptations which surround us. Be thou merciful, Oh Heavenly Father! to Creatures so formed & situated.*

*We bless thee for every comfort of our past and present existence, for our health of Body & of Mind & for every other source of happiness which Thou hast bountifully bestowed on us & with which we close this day, imploring their continuance from Thy Fatherly goodness, with a more grateful sense* of them, than they have hitherto excited. May the comforts of every day, be thankfully felt by us, may they prompt a willing obedience of thy Commandments & a benevolent spirit towards every fellow–creature.

Have Mercy Oh Gracious Father! upon all that are now suffering from whatsoever cause, that are in any circumstance of danger or distress. Give them patience under every affliction, strengthen, comfort & relieve them. To Thy Goodness we commend ourselves this night beseeching thy protection of us through its darkness & dangers. We are helpless & dependent; Graciously preserve us. For all whom we love & value, for every Friend & Connection, we equally pray; However divided & far asunder, we know that we are alike before Thee, & under thine Eye. May we be equally united in Thy Faith & Fear, in fervent devotion towards Thee, & in Thy merciful Protection this night. Pardon Oh Lord! the imperfections of these our Prayers, & accept them through the mediation of our Blessed Saviour, in whose Holy Words, we further address thee;

Our Father . . .

—Jane Austen

# *Day 11*

## LOOK DOWN WITH FAVOR

*Almighty God! Look down with Mercy on thy Servants here assembled & accept the petitions now offered up unto thee.*

In this opening line of her second prayer, Jane asks God to look down with mercy and favor as she and her family gather to pray. Her words and tone convey a strong belief in a loving, personal God who "sits above the circle of the earth" (Isaiah 40:22) and yet is close at hand. She asks God to "look down with Mercy" and "accept the petitions" they offer. Jane's words paint a picture of a group of children gathering to talk to their father as he comes close to listen.

In his *Memoir*, James Edward Austen-Leigh describes the land around the parsonage at Steventon, Jane's home until she was twenty-five:

Two . . . hedgerows radiated, as it were, from the parsonage garden. One, a continuation of the turf terrace, proceeded westward, forming the southern boundary of the home meadows; and was formed into a rustic shrubbery, with occasional seats, entitled "The Wood Walk." The other ran straight up the hill, under the name of "The Church Walk," because it led to the parish church.[1]

It's lovely to imagine this scene from a bird's-eye view, with the Lord "looking down" on it from above. There, in a tiny village in the heart of England's Hampshire, a rectory sits, bursting with life and laughter. On the "warm southern side" there is a "walled garden with its sundial, espaliered fruit trees, vegetable and flower beds and grassy walks."[2] Green meadows stretch beyond it, dotted with livestock. Inside the house, in the evening, a family gathers to pray.

For the eyes of the Lord are on the righteous, and his ears are open to their prayer.
—1 Peter 3:12

In the Bible, believers gather to pray throughout the New Testament. Jesus got up early and went to desolate places to pray, Paul and Silas prayed and sang in jail, and the Epistles speak often of the prayers by and for the brethren. As Christians, we are exhorted to "pray without ceasing" (1 Thessalonians 5:17), to "pray for one another" (James 5:16), to pray together (Acts 1:14), and to pray on our own "in secret" (Matthew 6:6).

Jane's prayer reminds us that we can come close to God in prayer, whenever and wherever. Jane's father taught his children to "'say their prayers' (as the phrase went) night and morning, thanking God for the blessings they had received and humbly seeking his continued protection."[3] When we pray, God sees us and hears us. The world is not so big, nor the people in it so numerous, that he does not know each one of us personally. He not only calls us by name (Isaiah 43:1), he knows the number of hairs on our heads (Luke 12:7).

This is the wonder of God the Father: While he watches over all of creation, he simultaneously cares for each of us personally. When we "draw near to God," he draws near to us (James 4:8). When we call on God, he hears, he works, he moves. He "look[s] down with Mercy" when we come to him in prayer.

But truly God has listened; he has attended to the voice of my prayer. Blessed be God, because he has not rejected my prayer or removed his steadfast love from me!

—Psalm 66:19–20

### Invitation to Pray

The hedgerows at Jane's childhood home led in two directions: "The Wood Walk" down toward the lower meadows and "The Church Walk" up toward the church. Metaphorically, the "church walk" is perhaps the most obvious path to prayer. Corporate prayer with other believers is a key ingredient to a vibrant prayer life. Incredible things happen when we gather to pray at specific times and at appointed places.

However, "The Wood Walk" of personal prayer is also necessary for a balanced and powerful prayer life. When we spend extended time in prayer each day and "pray without ceasing" as we walk, drive, work, and play, we grow in our relationship with Christ and experience spiritual fruit in our lives. Take this time now to enjoy a quiet time of prayer.

### Let Us Pray

*Almighty God, thank you for reminding me today that you see and hear me when I pray. I want to have a fruitful, Spirit-led prayer life. Please show me when and where I can gather to pray with other Christians, either with a friend or a prayer group. Please help me to grow in my personal prayers as well. I need your help in this area of my prayer life: [your specific needs]. In Jesus' name, Amen.*

I call upon you, for you will answer me,
O God; incline your ear to me;
hear my words.
—Psalm 17:6

# *Day 12*

## MAKE US MINDFUL

*Pardon Oh God! the offences of the past day. We are conscious of many frailties; we remember with shame & contrition, many evil Thoughts & neglected duties, & we have perhaps sinned against Thee & against our fellow–creatures in many instances of which we have now no remembrance.*

Jane now enters into a time of recollection and confession in her prayer. While morning prayer lends itself to seeking God's direction for the day, evening prayer often focuses on looking back over the day in personal reflection. As Jane considers her day, she asks God's pardon (or forgiveness) for any "offences," "evil Thoughts," "neglected duties," or sins.

Jane's life, faith, and writing were undoubtedly influenced by the prayers in the Church of England's *Book of Common Prayer*. Jane heard these prayers at home and at church, read them for herself, and learned many of them by heart. She not only understood the spiritual meaning of the prayers, she knew the heft and rhythm of their lines and phrases. The content and the cadences undoubtedly spoke to her spiritual nature *and* to her writer's ear.

This portion of Jane's prayer bears a striking similarity to one of the evening prayers in the *Book of Common Prayer* which says, "We have left undone those things which we ought to have done; And we have done those things which we ought not to have done; And there is no health in us."[1] Similarly, Jane's prayer recognizes that we can have no health in us when our days are littered with unconfessed sin and offense.

> For when I kept silent [about my sin],
> my bones wasted away through my groaning all day long. For day and night your hand was heavy upon me; my strength was dried up as by the heat of summer.
> —Psalm 32:3–4

Reflection and confession bring about restoration—with God and with man. First, as we confess our sins and offenses, God forgives us and cleanses us: "If we confess our sins, he is faithful and just to forgive us our sins and to cleanse us from all unrighteousness" (1 John 1:9). Second, reflection paves the way for right relationships with the people around us.

The Bible says that sin, like yeast, will spread if left unattended: "Don't you realize that this sin is like a little yeast that spreads through the whole batch of dough?" (1 Corinthians 5:6 NIV). If we allow even a little bit of sin to go unchecked, it starts to permeate every part of our lives. Little slivers of bitterness, jealousy, or selfish ambition don't stay small for long; they grow and seep into every part of our thoughts, motives, words, and actions.

Jane's prayer echoes the theme of these verses. When we let the minor "offences" of our day go unnoticed—the petty remarks, the rolled eyes, the sighs, and the short words—we lose our spiritual sensitivity to the things that grieve the Holy Spirit. The things we say (publicly or secretly) and the attitudes we harbor start to affect who we are and become part of the tapestry of our lives. Jane's prayer reminds us that when we become sloppy in our relationship with God or with others, disunity, disharmony, and discord will abound.

I acknowledged my sin to you, and I did not cover my iniquity; I said, "I will confess my transgressions to the Lord," and you forgave the iniquity of my sin.
—Psalm 32:5

### Invitation to Pray

Is there unconfessed sin or a bitter attitude lingering in your life? Have you harbored negative thoughts or neglected a duty? Maybe you slighted a friend or snapped at your spouse. Perhaps there is someone you need to forgive. Unconfessed sin is similar to having a splinter: If you leave it alone, it will fester; once you take it out, there's relief.

Confession is simply agreeing with God. Ask him to show you the nooks and crannies of your heart that need tending. Take this time now to come to the Lord in quiet reflection and confession, just as Jane did, and lay everything at his feet. As you pray, ask God to restore and refresh your spirit.

### Let Us Pray

*Heavenly Father, thank you for loving me. I want to take this time to reflect carefully on my day. I come to you with a humble heart, laying before you my offenses and sins, my frailties, negative thoughts, and neglected duties. Open my eyes to anything that's amiss in my relationship with you or another person. Please forgive me for: [your specific confession]. Please help me restore my relationship with: [specific name]. In Jesus' name, Amen.*

Blessed is the one whose transgression
is forgiven, whose sin is covered.
—Psalm 32:1

# Day 13

## INVADE OUR HABITS

*Pardon Oh God! whatever thou hast seen amiss in us, & give us a stronger desire of resisting every evil inclination & weakening every habit of sin.*

In Caroline Austen's book *My Aunt Jane: A Memoir*, she describes Jane's morning habits: "Aunt Jane began her day with music . . . before breakfast—when she could have the room to herself—She practised regularly every morning—She played very pretty tunes, I thought . . . but the music (for I knew the books well in after years) would now be thought disgracefully easy."[1]

Habits form the structure of our lives and days—what we do, how we spend our time, what we eat, where we go, and even when we go to bed and when we rise. Jane's habit of practicing the piano each morning is intriguing. From Caroline's account, Jane did not play new or difficult songs. She practiced, it seems, because she liked to start the day "with music." Furthermore, she most likely enjoyed it as a time of reflection and contemplation.

In this portion of Jane's prayer, she focuses on spiritual habits. She asks God to give her "a stronger desire" to resist "every evil inclination" and weaken "every habit of sin." Her words echo many New Testament Scriptures that speak about the importance of training ourselves spiritually. Specifically, the apostle Paul uses physical training as a metaphor for spiritual training, likening the spiritual life to a race and the believer to a runner (1 Corinthians 9:24).

> Have nothing to do with irreverent, silly myths. Rather train yourself for godliness; for while bodily training is of some value, godliness is of value in every way, as it holds promise for the present life and also for the life to come.
> —1 Timothy 4:7–8

Jesus himself had a rhythm to his day and often rose early to "withdraw" from the pressing crowds—and indeed his own disciples—in order to pray (Luke 5:16). The word *withdraw* means to "retire quietly" or "go aside."[2] The foundational habit of Jesus' life was prayer: at the start of the day, throughout the day, for the people around him, and before making any decisions.

Just as Jane's day began with purpose and rhythm, her life and week also exhibited a spiritual pattern of discipline and holiness. Her faith undergirded the way she lived and moved through life. Her novels and family documents speak of the high value Jane put on moral integrity, spiritual devotedness, and character growth. Her life was lived simply and openly, and her weekly routine included regular church attendance, prayer, and Bible reading.

Jane's prayer reminds us to ask God if anything is "amiss" in our lives and priorities. Many of us try to fit God into our lives, instead of making God the centerpiece of our lives. Giving our first fruits to God isn't just about money; it's also about our time. One beneficial daily habit is to begin each day with prayer and Bible reading. Regular attendance at church for services, Bible studies, and small groups are fruitful weekly habits. As you seek God first, you will experience steady growth in your relationship with him.

For to set the mind on the flesh is death, but to set the mind on the Spirit is life and peace.
—Romans 8:6

### Invitation to Pray

What do you spend your time doing? Which habits and activities bring you closer to Jesus and stir your faith and which cause spiritual apathy and disinterest? One way we can move closer to God and away from sinful habits is to exchange old habits for new. As you turn from activities that weaken your resolve and do things that help you draw closer to God, your desire for the things of God grows.

You can feed your spirit by spending time in God's Word and in prayer, by using your gifts and talents to serve Jesus, and by learning from mature believers. Take this time now to pray over your habits and routines. If you see habitual sin in your life, invite God in and ask him to strengthen you and give you a "stronger desire of resisting every evil inclination."

### *Let Us Pray*

*Dear Jesus, thank you for this reminder that habits matter. I want to be more like you and build up my spiritual life. Please open my eyes to the habits that feed my flesh and the habits that stir and refresh my soul and spirit. Help me change my routine and make you the center of my life. I often try to fit you into my schedule instead of building my life around you. Please help me to evaluate my habits: [your specific needs]. In Jesus' name, Amen.*

But seek first the kingdom of God and
his righteousness, and all these things
will be added to you.
—Matthew 6:33

# *Day 14*

## GUARD OUR HEARTS

*Thou knowest the infirmity of our Nature, & the temptations which surround us. Be thou merciful, Oh Heavenly Father! to Creatures so formed & situated.*

In *Sense and Sensibility*, Elinor and Marianne are quite different in their outlook on life, their opinions, and their emotional makeup. Where Elinor is sensible and level-headed, Marianne is romantic, full of feeling, and sees the world in full color. However, though they are unalike in many ways, Elinor and Marianne know one another uniquely and intimately.

When Willoughby bursts onto the scene, full of "youth, beauty, and elegance," interested in her sister, Elinor is immediately on guard.[1] She knows the "infirmity of [Marianne's] Nature," her weaknesses, and her temptations. Elinor is wary of Marianne's quick attachment to Willoughby as he steadily becomes her "most exquisite enjoyment."[2] Elinor watches, she waits, she cautions.

And when everything eventually falls apart, she consoles and comforts.

Jane's prayer reminds us that God knows *our* unique weaknesses and frailties, that he knows "the infirmity of our Nature, & the temptations which surround us" better than anyone else. He gave us our breath and spirit (Isaiah 42:5) and knows our emotional makeup, our thoughts, our past, our failures, our habits, and our perceptions. He knows our blind spots and the things that are likely to turn our heads and catch our eyes. Jane comes to her "Heavenly Father," to the one who knows her best, to ask for his compassion on "Creatures so formed & situated."

> As a father shows compassion to his children, so the Lord shows compassion to those who fear him. For he knows our frame; he remembers that we are dust.
> —Psalm 103:13–14

We read that Willoughby is "*exactly formed* to engage Marianne's heart" (emphasis mine).[3] And the same is true for each of us: We are each susceptible to certain people and things that are "exactly formed" to capture our unique interests and attractions. Just as Marianne delights in Willoughby's "good abilities, quick imagination, lively spirits, and open, affectionate manners,"[4] we each delight in specific character traits, personalities, and aesthetics.

The Bible says, "No temptation has overtaken you that is not common to man" (1 Corinthians 10:13). It also says that all temptation stems from one of three core issues: "the desires of the flesh and the desires of the eyes and pride of life" (1 John 2:16). The desires of the flesh consist of sinful activities that focus on physical and emotional pleasure. The desires of the eyes concern anything sinful we view or anything we covet with our eyes. Lastly, the pride of life comes in the form of success and the desire for importance, privilege, and power.

Guarding our hearts is essential in the face of temptation. Just as Jane prayed for God's mercy on "Creatures so formed," we can ask for God's help in our weak spots. Jesus tells us exactly what to do to guard our hearts: "Watch and pray that you may not enter into temptation. The spirit indeed is willing, but the flesh is weak" (Matthew 26:41). Rather than play of-

> How can a young man keep his way pure? By guarding it according to your word.
> —Psalm 119:9

fense when temptations hit, we need to play defense and guard our eyes and ears from the things that can pollute our minds and hearts.

## Invitation to Pray

Temptation manifests itself in a myriad of subtle ways. The desire of the flesh often disguises itself as a juicy piece of gossip, a tasty treat, a puff of smoke, or a vent of anger. The desire of the eyes sometimes sneaks up when a friend moves into a new house, gets married, or has a baby. The pride of life can hit with a vengeance when we see someone doing the work we want to do or getting the accolades we want to hear.

Guarding our hearts includes thinking carefully about what we listen to, look at, watch, and read, as well as who we spend time with. It's important to pray for discernment, asking God to show us the people and activities that draw us closer to God and those that push us away and distract us. As you pray now, ask God to help you see your vulnerabilities and guard your heart.

### Let Us Pray

*Heavenly Father, you know me through and through. I don't have to hide from you. Instead, I can come to you anytime, anywhere. Lord, make me aware of the situations that spark my temptations and help me to avoid them. Please purify my heart and my mind. Show me what Bible verse I can store in my mind today. I ask now for your mercy and help in this area of temptation: [your specific needs]. In Jesus' name, Amen.*

Above all else, guard your heart,
for everything you do flows from it.
—Proverbs 4:23 NIV

# *Day 15*

## A GOOD FATHER

*We bless thee for every comfort of our past and present existence,
for our health of Body & of Mind & for every other source of
happiness which Thou hast bountifully bestowed on us & with
which we close this day, imploring their continuance from Thy
Fatherly goodness, with a more grateful sense of them, than they
have hitherto excited.*

By all accounts, Jane was a happy, content person. Upon attending a dance when she was 33 years old, she says this in a letter to Cassandra: "It was the same room in which we danced 15 years ago!—I thought it all over—& inspite [*sic*] of the shame of being so much older, felt with Thankfulness that I was quite as happy now as then."[1]

Some people are naturally lighthearted, and the Austens were known for having a happy nature and a cheerful outlook on life. However, this portion of Jane's prayer provides a clue to a deeper source of joy and contentment. It speaks to the foundation of her life and mindset: a firm belief in God's "Fatherly goodness." In these lines, Jane thanks God for the comforts of her "past and present existence," for "health of Body & of Mind," and for "every other source of happiness." She asks God to continue his goodness toward her and for "a more grateful sense" of the blessings in her life.

Jane's prayer reminds us that when we set our minds on our present comforts and our past blessings, our perspective on today and tomorrow shifts. When we meditate on all that God has done and is doing, hope for tomorrow stirs, faith expands, and our belief in God's kindness and "Fatherly goodness" grows.

> See what great love the Father has lavished on us, that we should be called children of God! And that is what we are!
> —I John 3:1 NIV

If Jane danced in that room 15 years earlier, she would have been 18 at the time. Years later, Jane is older and wiser (and still single), yet she retains her pleasant view of life. She enjoys the dance and is neither bitter nor depressed. She even quips about a gentleman's eyes, saying they "may be the best part of him."[2] Jane seems as happy as ever, enjoying life and its amusing moments.

When we trust in God's "Fatherly goodness" and pursue a close relationship with him, we find contentment. Jane was neither rich nor famous in her lifetime. She lived a quiet life that revolved around family and close friends. However, Jane's prayer points us to the underlying focus of her life—a "grateful sense" of God's faithfulness.

We can cultivate this same "grateful sense" of God's goodness by actively looking for his blessings in the finer details of our lives. When we take note of "every comfort of our past and present existence," every bit of "health of Body & of Mind," and "every other source of happiness" God has "bountifully bestowed on us," our hearts swell with gratitude.

Your love, Lord,
reaches to the
heavens, your
faithfulness
to the skies.
—Psalm 36:5 NIV

### Invitation to Pray

Are there special blessings and comforts God has provided in your life? Take this time to reflect on God's goodness, both in the good times and the bad. Thank him for his faithfulness to guide, heal, comfort, and love you in every season.

Or perhaps you're struggling to trust God's fatherly goodness as you face what feels like an impossible situation or insurmountable problem. Take heart! Just as God brought Abraham out of the desert, the Israelites out of Egypt, Joseph out of the prison, Daniel out of the lion's den, and David out of adultery, God will bring you out, too. Jesus came out of the tomb and conquered death. He will defeat your enemies as well. Start today by asking him to defeat hopelessness and restore joy in your heart.

### Let Us Pray

*Thank you, God, for your kindness and your fatherly goodness. Thank you for the many comforts and blessings you've provided in my life. Please help me to see the simple, everyday wonders of your love and faithfulness. I want to know you more. I lift up to you now those things that steal my joy and weigh me down: [your specific needs]. I love you, Lord. Thank you for loving me. In Jesus' name, Amen.*

Know therefore that the Lord your God
is God, the faithful God who keeps covenant
and steadfast love with those who love him
and keep his commandments,
to a thousand generations.
—Deuteronomy 7:9

# Day 16

## A BENEVOLENT SPIRIT

*May the comforts of every day, be thankfully felt by us, may they prompt a willing obedience of thy Commandments & a benevolent spirit toward every fellow–creature.*

By all accounts, Jane did embody a "benevolent spirit toward every fellow-creature," in her relationships with her friends, acquaintances, and family. She was particularly loving toward her nieces and nephews. It doesn't appear that Jane's writing schedule or personal agenda ruled her life or her days or that she was annoyed by the talk, play, or presence of small children. In fact, quite the reverse seems true. Jane was generous with her time and her talents.

Austen family letters and memoirs show that Jane was a loving and affectionate aunt who enjoyed family life and entertained the children in her family with "the most delightful stories, chiefly of Fairy-land," in which "her fairies had all characters of their own."[1]

And though she wrote quite prolifically in the latter part of her life, she still spent time with her family and was reportedly "the general favourite with children; her ways with them being so playful, and her long circumstantial stories so delightful."[2]

This portion of Jane's prayer points to a natural desire to *act* on the many comforts God has given. Jane prays that the blessings she's received will prompt a "willing obedience" toward God and "a benevolent spirit" toward others. Jane's prayer echoes Jesus' teaching and way of life during his earthly ministry and the two great commandments he gave to his followers.

And he said to him, "You shall love the Lord your God with all your heart and with all your soul and with all your mind. This is the great and first commandment. And a second is like it: You shall love your neighbor as yourself."

—Matthew 22:37–39

Jesus' life provides us the ultimate example of obedience to God and love for people. Wherever he went, he healed broken bodies, filled empty stomachs, and brought the dead to life. He invested in the lives of people of all ages, from every walk of life, including little children, saying "Let the little children come to me" (Matthew 19:14). Jesus "came not to be served but to serve, and to give his life as a ransom for many" (Matthew 20:28).

Jesus' obedience to the Father extended even unto death: "Father, if you are willing, remove this cup from me. Nevertheless, not my will, but yours, be done" (Luke 22:42). He ultimately expressed his love for mankind when he gave his life as a ransom for sin, so those who would believe in him could receive the forgiveness of sin and eternal life with God (John 3:16). When we think of all that Christ gave for us so that we could be saved, it stirs up "a benevolent spirit" in our hearts. And when we bless others, we in turn are blessed.

Jane's prayer reminds us to pray for "a willing obedience" toward God and "a benevolent spirit" toward others. Spending time with her nieces and nephews is just one tangible way Jane expressed that loving, "benevolent spirit": "Her first charm to children was great sweetness of manner. She seemed to love you, and you loved her in return."[3] The time she invested in each of their lives, both as children and as adults, was not forgotten. After she passed away, several of them wrote about the example she set for them as a Christian, as an author, and as an aunt.

> Whoever brings blessing will be enriched, and one who waters will himself be watered.
> —Proverbs 11:25

## Invitation to Pray

Is there an area of your heart that shrinks back from a wholehearted, full-bodied love for God? Is there any area of obedience that has become routine or even grudging in your life? Take this time today to pray about the practical ways you can love and obey God with all of your heart, mind, soul, and strength.

Is there someone in your life who needs more of your time, love, and attention? Or someone toward whom you don't feel very benevolent? Take this time to pray about the "fellow-creature" God might want you to spend time with today. It might be a neighbor, a friend, or a child or grandchild who needs your time or your help. You never know the ripple effect your generosity can have in another person's life as you give of the time, talent, and treasure God has given to you.

### Let Us Pray

*Lord God, thank you for all that you've given me. I want to respond by obeying you more fully and by loving others more generously. Please make me more like Jesus in how I relate to you and to the people around me. Make me a generous giver with all that you've provided: my money, my time, and my talents. I need your help in this area of reluctant obedience or generosity: [your specific needs]. In Jesus' name, Amen.*

Do not neglect to do good and to share
what you have, for such sacrifices
are pleasing to God.
—Hebrews 13:16

# *Day 17*

## GIVE US PATIENCE

*Have Mercy Oh Gracious Father! upon all that are now suffering from whatsoever cause, that are in any circumstance of danger or distress. Give them patience under every affliction, strengthen, comfort & relieve them.*

This portion of Jane's prayer is a prayer of intercession. In it, Jane prays on behalf of "all" who are suffering or are "in any circumstance of danger or distress." Her words reflect her confidence in God's ability to strengthen us during times of pain and trial, comfort us in our seasons of deepest need, provide us with his tangible help and presence in life's hardest moments, and give us "patience under every affliction."

In *Mansfield Park*, Fanny experiences distress on a daily basis. She has no voice, her opinions are misunderstood, and her wishes are disregarded. Her little attic room and her conversations with Edmund are her only refuge. She exists in a kind of middle-world between servant and family member, "carrying messages, and fetching" what others want.[1] She suffers from various causes of loneliness and heartache throughout much of the novel.

Yet Fanny Price closely embodies the kind of patience under affliction Jane writes about in her prayer. Despite her troubles, Fanny has an inner strength and fortitude that never lags. Though she is mistreated and suffers in mind, body, and soul at times, she finds solace in her little attic room and in quiet reflection. She doesn't lash out or become bitter. Even in the face of disappointment and anxiety, she quietly waits and hopes.

Be joyful in hope, patient in affliction, faithful in prayer.
—Romans 12:12 NIV

In the Old Testament, Joseph experiences distress beyond what most of us can imagine. His brothers sell him into slavery and tell his parents he died, but when Joseph is sold to Potiphar, God raises him up to the position of manager in charge of "everything in [Potiphar's] entire household" (Genesis 39:8 NLT). Then, when Potiphar's wife falsely accuses Joseph of attacking her and he's put in prison, the Lord is "with Joseph," showing him "steadfast love" and giving him "favor in the sight of the keeper of the prison" (Genesis 39:21). Later, when he is forgotten in prison for two years, God enables him to interpret Pharaoh's dream. He is released from prison and saves the Egyptians and his own family from starvation (Genesis 41–47).

When Joseph's brothers sold him, he took nothing with him except his faith in God. In every difficult situation, God was with

Joseph, working in his life for good, using even the worst circumstances in Joseph's life for a purpose: "As for you, you meant evil against me, but God meant it for good, to bring it about that many people should be kept alive, as they are today" (Genesis 50:20).

Jane's prayer for "patience under every affliction" and for strength, comfort, and relief in distress is based on biblical truth: The Bible says God "gives power to the faint" (Isaiah 40:29), he is the "God of all comfort" (2 Corinthians 1:3), and he gives us "relief from [our] suffering" (Isaiah 14:3 NIV). In this broken world, we face illness, danger, and grief, but in everything, God is with us. When trouble comes, we can pray for God's favor to descend, for his presence to come, and for his love to pour out.

> But you, O Lord, are a shield about me, my glory, and the lifter of my head.
> —Psalm 3:3

### Invitation to Pray

Have you ever felt like Joseph— alone, enslaved, or forgotten? Are you suffering or in any kind of distress today? Let Joseph's story encourage you that God is with you and has a plan and a purpose for your life. Take this time to pray and ask God for patience, strength, comfort, and refreshment *in* your affliction.

Or perhaps you know someone experiencing a painful trial. God invites you to bring Jesus to that person. You can send a card, write out a Bible verse, and call or visit. When you take someone's hand and pray for his or her needs, God gives spiritual, emotional, and mental relief.

### Let Us Pray

*Thank you, God, that you are an ever-present help in my times of need. Thank you that you are strength, comfort, and relief. I now lift up to you the things that are distressing in my life: [your specific needs]. I also lift up to you the people I know who are suffering or in a difficult trial: [specific names]. Please show me who I can reach out to today with a phone call, a Bible verse, and a time of prayer. In Jesus' name, Amen.*

Blessed be the God and Father of our Lord
Jesus Christ, the Father of mercies and
God of all comfort, who comforts us in all
our affliction, so that we may be able to
comfort those who are in any affliction,
with the comfort with which
we ourselves are comforted by God.
—2 Corinthians 1:3–4

# *Day 18*

## KEEP THE NIGHT WATCHES

*To Thy Goodness we commend ourselves this night beseeching thy*
*protection of us through its darkness & dangers.*

During her first night at Northanger Abbey, Catherine Morland's imagination gets the better of her. In the old, dark, and drafty house, with a storm raging outside, it doesn't take much for the fanciful Catherine to lose her nerve. When she goes to her chamber at the end of the evening, she enters "her room with a tolerably stout heart."[1] However, once her fire dies down and her candle goes out, Catherine's bravery quickly dissolves:

> A lamp could not have expired with more awful effect. Catherine, for a few moments, was motionless with horror. It was done completely; not a remnant of light in the wick could give hope to the rekindling breath. Darkness impenetrable and immovable filled the room. A violent gust of wind, rising with sudden fury, added fresh horror to the moment.[2]

85

Catherine jumps into bed, creeps "far" under the blankets, and is unable to sleep until the storm dies down.

Though we as readers know that Catherine is in no actual danger, this humorous scene points to an important question: When we're in the dark and storms rage in our lives, where do we run for help? This portion of Jane's prayer speaks to life's "darkness & dangers." Many people today experience various forms of anxiety and worry. Jane's prayer reminds us to "commend" ourselves to God's goodness, putting our lives into his care and keeping.

Jane may have prayed this prayer of protection because she feared some real danger in her small village. More likely, she prayed these lines because she knew what most of us know: Things always seem worse at night. Fear and anxiety build as life winds down, people drift off to sleep, and the house grows quiet. We obsess over the situations we can't control and the problems we can't solve. Our thoughts wander and minor issues grow out of proportion.

> When he calls to me, I will answer him; I will be with him in trouble; I will rescue him and honor him.
>
> —Psalm 91:15

Jane's prayer reminds us to "commend" ourselves to God and "beseech" his physical and spiritual protection in our lives and in the lives of those we love. The Bible is filled with verses to help us battle fear because God knows that when the darkness comes, either literally or figuratively, it can easily press in and overwhelm us. He invites us to know him and trust him. Psalm 46:10 says, "Be still, and know that I am God."

When you're confused or anxious, you can turn to God's Word; it's a "lamp" for your feet and a "light" to your path (Psalm 119:105). "The name of the Lord is a strong tower" (Proverbs 18:10), he never sleeps (Psalm 121:4), and his angels guard his people (Psalm 91:11). When you're surrounded by trouble, you can pray and sing like Paul and Silas did in jail (Acts 16:23–25). God is your rescue (Psalm 140:1) and your refuge (Psalm 46:1). In life's darkness and storms, we can cower under the covers or we can stand firm in prayer.

You are a hiding place for me; you preserve me from trouble; you surround me with shouts of deliverance.
—Psalm 32:7

### Invitation to Pray

Most of us struggle with fear in some way or at certain times in our lives. We worry about bodily harm to us, our family members, or our children. We imagine frightening scenarios and think of scary what-ifs. But God says, "Fear not, for I am with you; be not dismayed, for I am your God; I will strengthen you, I will help you, I will uphold you with my righteous right hand" (Isaiah 41:10).

God doesn't want to saddle you with the burden of fear. Fear is an emotion that traps you inside your thoughts and keeps you from living in freedom. Take this time now to ask God to be your hiding place, your strong tower, your shield, and your protector.

### Let Us Pray

*Almighty God, thank you for promising to protect me. I feel anxious when I hear upsetting stories from friends and relatives and on the news. Our world is so broken, and I confess that I am often fearful. I ask you now to please lift the weight of fear from my shoulders. It's too heavy for me. I give it to you now, Lord. Please open my eyes to your power to help in this area of my life: [your specific needs]. In Jesus' name, Amen.*

I remember you upon my bed,
and meditate on you in the watches of the
night; for you have been my help, and in the
shadow of your wings I will sing for joy.
—Psalm 63:6–7

# Day 19

## TO THE FARTHEST REACHES

*We are helpless & dependent; Graciously preserve us. For all whom we love & value, for every Friend & Connection, we equally pray; However divided & far asunder, we know that we are alike before Thee, & under thine Eye.*

Jane's letters to her sister, Cassandra, are long and full of detail. To save postage, people in Jane's day wrote horizontally across the page until it was filled, then turned the paper ninety degrees and wrote across it again. Sometimes, they even turned the paper one more time and wrote across the sheet upside-down. It's easy to imagine what joy Cassandra felt when she received a letter from Jane that began with "My dearest Cassandra" and was filled with lines and lines of news.

In this portion of her prayer, Jane prays for those whom she loves and values, for "every Friend & Connection," and for those "divided & far asunder." For Jane, this most likely included praying for her brothers in the navy, for any family who were traveling, and for friends and family who lived in other parts of the country. She asks God to keep them "under" his watchful eye of protection.

Faithfulness in prayer is difficult, especially if we don't see someone regularly. Even our closest friends, family members, and coworkers can quickly become "out of sight, out of mind" if they move away, switch churches, or change jobs. As Jane and Cassandra's letters prove, staying close requires frequent interaction. In the same way, it takes time, communication, and diligence to pray for those we love, particularly if they are "far asunder."

Moreover, as for me, far be it from me that I should sin against the Lord by ceasing to pray for you, and I will instruct you in the good and the right way.

—1 Samuel 12:23

The apostle Paul wrote lengthy letters to the Christians in the cities he had visited because he loved them, was concerned for them, and missed them. In them, he says he prays for the Romans "without ceasing" (1:9), for the Colossians "always" (1:3), and for the Thessalonians "constantly" (1 Thessalonians 1:2). He does "not cease to give thanks" for the Ephesians (Ephesians 1:16) and prays for Timothy "night and day" (2 Timothy 1:3). Wherever Paul found himself—whether on a missionary journey, shipwrecked on an island, or in a prison—he prayed for those he loved without stopping.

Jane's prayer echoes Paul's letters and reminds us to pray for those we love, both near and far. The visual of Regency letters is a lovely picture of thoroughly covering someone in prayer. First, we can pray for the "horizontal" life of those we love—for the things they do, the places they go, the work they do, and their safety, health, and influences. Next, we can turn our attention to the "vertical" part of their lives—praying for their relationship with God, their desire to please him, their interest and investment in spiritual growth, and their passion for his Word.

We can then "rotate" our prayers again and move into a time of prayer for their future, their purpose, and their service. We can pray for them to be stirred up by the Holy Spirit to good works, that they would fan into flame and exercise their spiritual gifts, and that they would be called into a life of personal ministry and be shown their purpose and calling in this world.

> I thank my God in all my remembrance of you, always in every prayer of mine for you all making my prayer with joy.
> —Philippians 1:3–4

### Invitation to Pray

Jane's prayer reminds us of the need for consistent prayer. Is there someone you want to pray for regularly who is "far asunder," either geographically or spiritually? Consider writing that person's name down on a note card and praying for his or her personal, practical, and spiritual needs daily.

One of the best and most powerful ways to pray for someone is to pray Bible verses for him or her. You can do this with almost any verse, but the Psalms, Proverbs, and New Testament Epistles are especially suited to this type of prayer. Consider praying all of Ephesians 3:14–19 for a friend or family member by simply praying the verses out loud and inserting his or her name for each pronoun.

### Let Us Pray

*Lord, thank you for this important reminder to stand in the gap and pray on behalf of others. Please make me faithful, consistent, and thorough in my prayers. Teach me to be an intercessor. Please show me who I should pray for today. I lift up to you those who are near: [insert specific names/needs here]. I also lift up to you those at a distance: [insert specific names/needs here]. In Jesus' name, Amen.*

For this reason I bow my knees before
the Father . . . that according to the riches of
his glory he may grant you to be strengthened
with power through his Spirit in your inner
being, so that Christ may dwell
in your hearts through faith.
—Ephesians 3:14, 16–17

# *Day 20*
# A FERVENT FAITH

*May we be equally united in Thy Faith & Fear, in fervent devotion
towards Thee, & in Thy merciful Protection this night.*

When we think of fervent devotion in Jane's novels, Anne
Elliot and Captain Wentworth come to mind. Though
they fall "rapidly and deeply in love,"[1] Anne is pressured to break
their engagement and Wentworth goes to sea. Years pass, but they
never stop loving each other. Captain Wentworth tries to forget
Anne but has "never seen a woman since whom he thought her
equal"[2] and has only "imagined himself indifferent."[3]

As for Anne, she regrets giving him up and wishes she had
acted differently: "No one had ever come within the Kellynch
circle, who could bear a comparison with Frederick Wentworth,
as he stood in her memory."[4] When they finally reunite, they are
"more exquisitely happy, perhaps, in their re-union, than when it
had been first projected."[5] Anne and Wentworth do not have a

lukewarm kind of affection for one another. Their love has been tested by fire; it is fervent and devoted.

In this portion of Jane's prayer, she prays for a "fervent devotion" toward God. Her words speak of a fiery kind of faith that doesn't grow cold or indifferent. It's a love that holds up under pressure and stands the test of time. Jane prays for passionate "Faith & Fear" (or reverence) toward God, not halfhearted or indifferent religious activity, reminding us that devotion to God can and should be our primary passion.

> I know your works, that you are neither cold nor hot. I could wish you were cold or hot. . . . you are lukewarm, and neither cold nor hot . . .
> —Revelation 3:15–16 NKJV

Jane isn't merely using beautiful, descriptive, or emotional language in her prayer. She is actually hitting on a deeper biblical truth: the dangerous issue of lukewarm faith. In 1 Kings 18, several generations after Israel split off from Judah, God sends the prophet Elijah to warn King Ahab and the Israelite people about their Baal worship. In a dramatic showdown between Elijah and Ahab and his false prophets, Elijah asks the people, "How long will you go limping between two different opinions? If the Lord is God, follow him; but if Baal, then follow him" (1 Kings 18:21). The Israelites' response: silence.

So Elijah stages the ultimate showdown with the 450 prophets of Baal: Both sides sacrifice a bull and lay it on wood, but they don't light a fire. The false prophets call to Baal, sure he will send down fire, praying "from morning to noon," even cutting themselves until they bleed, but the result is dismal: "There was no voice, and no one answered" (v. 26).

Finally, Elijah steps forward, calls all the people to come to him, and they do (v. 30). He takes twelve stones, builds an altar, digs a trench around it, and prepares the wood and the bull. He pours water over it all until everything is soaked and the trench is filled. Elijah prays, "Answer me, O Lord, answer me, that this people may know that you, O Lord, are God, and that you have turned their hearts back" (v. 37). The fire of the Lord falls and consumes the bull, the wood, the stones, the dust, and even the water in the trench. The Israelites' response: fiery faith!

### Invitation to Pray

Jane's prayer prompts an important question: Are you "limping between two different opinions" as the Israelites were, or are you following God with "fervent devotion"? If you're a Christian but realize you've grown lukewarm or even cool in your faith, take this time now to pray and renew your commitment to Christ.

> And when all the people saw it, they fell on their faces and said, "The Lord, he is God; the Lord, he is God."
> —1 Kings 18:39

Or you might find yourself wavering between a few religious beliefs, unsure of what you believe. Like the Israelites, we all have to decide who we will serve: God or anything else. Today is the day to draw near and choose to serve the "King of kings" (Revelation 19:16). If you would like to ask Jesus into your heart today as your personal Savior, there is a Special Invitation at the end of this book on page 146 where you can learn about how to do that.

### Let Us Pray

*Thank you, Lord, for this time to reflect on what I believe and the state of my heart and faith. I want to be fully devoted to you. I don't want to waver or be tossed about by different ideas or ideologies. Please work in my heart and life to help me know you more and grow in my faith. I ask your forgiveness for my indifference or lukewarm attitude in this area: [your specific confession here]. Thank you for loving me. In Jesus' name, Amen.*

Let your heart therefore be wholly devoted to the Lord our God, to walk in His statutes and to keep His commandments, as at this day.
—1 Kings 8:61 NASB

# ❧ *Prayer Three* ❧

*F*ather of Heaven! whose goodness has brought us in safety to the close of this day, dispose our Hearts in fervent prayer. Another day is now gone, & added to those, for which we were before accountable. Teach us Almighty Father, to consider this solemn Truth, as we should do, that we may feel the importance of every day, & every hour as it passes, & earnestly strive to make a better use of what Thy Goodness may yet bestow on us, than we have done of the Time past.

Give us Grace to endeavour after a truly Christian Spirit to seek to attain that temper of Forbearance & Patience, of which our Blessed Saviour has set us the highest Example, and which, while it prepares us for the spiritual Happiness of the life to come, will secure to us the best enjoyment of what this world can give. Incline us Oh God! to think humbly of ourselves, to be severe only in the examination of our own conduct, to consider our fellow-creatures with kindness, & to judge of all they say & do with that Charity which we would desire from Men ourselves.

97

We thank thee with all our hearts for every gracious dispensation, for all the Blessings that have attended our Lives, for every
hour of safety, health & peace, of domestic comfort & innocent
enjoyment. We feel that we have been blessed far beyond any thing
that we have deserved; and though we cannot but pray for a continuance of all these Mercies, we acknowledge our unworthiness of
them and implore Thee to pardon the presumption of our desires.

Keep us Oh! Heavenly Father from Evil this night. Bring us
in safety to the beginning of another day & grant that we may rise
again with every serious & religious feeling which now directs us.

May thy mercy be extended over all Mankind, bringing the
Ignorant to the knowledge of thy Truth, awakening the Impenitent, touching the Hardened. Look with compassion upon the
afflicted of every condition, assuage the pangs of disease, comfort
the broken in spirit.

More particularly do we pray for the safety and welfare of our
own family & friends wheresoever dispersed, beseeching Thee to
avert from them all material & lasting Evil of Body or Mind; &
may we by the assistance of thy Holy Spirit so conduct ourselves
on Earth as to secure an Eternity of Happiness with each other
in thy Heavenly Kingdom. Grant this most merciful Father, for
the sake of our Blessed Saviour in whose Holy Name & Words
we further address Thee.

Our Father . . .

—Jane Austen

# *Day 21*

## FERVENT IN PRAYER

*Father of Heaven! whose goodness has brought us in safety to the close of this day, dispose our Hearts in fervent prayer.*

In *Mansfield Park*, the "handsome chapel" at Mr. Rushworth's estate was "formerly in constant use both morning and evening. Prayers were always read in it by the domestic chaplain, within the memory of many; but the late Mr. Rushworth left it off."[1] Miss Crawford quips that "every generation has its improvements,"[2] but Fanny responds passionately, saying it's a "pity" the chapel is no longer used for daily prayers: "There is something in a chapel and chaplain so much in character with a great house, with one's ideas of what such a household should be! A whole family assembling regularly for the purpose of prayer is fine!"[3]

While Fanny considers morning and evening prayers "a valuable part of former times,"[4] Miss Crawford says that the "obligation of attendance, the formality, the restraint, the length of time" is "a formidable thing, and what nobody likes."[5] At the crux of their argument is a difference of heart: To Miss Crawford, daily prayer is an empty ritual; to Fanny, corporate prayer and fellowship with other believers is a source of pleasure.

During Jane's lifetime, religious life had become, for many, a duty rather than a joy. However, we see in this opening line of her third prayer that Jane desired a "fervent" prayer life. She addresses her "Father of Heaven" with an exclamation, acknowledging his "goodness" and thanking him for another day spent "in safety." These lines do not suggest obligatory prayer; instead, they express deep feeling and joy.

> Happy are those who hear the joyful call to worship, for they will walk in the light of your presence, Lord. They rejoice all day long in your wonderful reputation. They exult in your righteousness.
> —Psalm 89:15–16 NLT

Jane probably didn't always feel like skipping up the lane to church on Sunday, especially on a muddy morning or when she had a cold. She most likely didn't experience a glorious rush of excitement every time she prayed. Thus, she begins this third prayer in the most wonderful and practical way: by asking God to "dispose" (or incline or position) her heart to be "fervent" in prayer.

Jane's words point to an important truth: Our hearts and minds are not naturally predisposed to fervency in prayer—or really anything. In fact, we don't even feel continually passionate about the people and things we love the most. In our marriages, we don't always *feel* the same overwhelming, romantic love that we felt when we first married. With our children, we don't *feel* the same gush of emotion each day that we did when they were born.

In reality, our hearts are actually more prone to apathy, lethargy, and even atrophy. The Bible points us to the key ingredient to maintaining a vibrant prayer life—praying "in the Spirit." Ephesians 6:18 says, "And pray in the Spirit on all occasions with all kinds of prayers and requests. With this in mind, be alert and always keep on praying for all the Lord's people" (NIV). Anyone can recite words, but when we ask the Holy Spirit to lead us, our prayers come to life.

Let my prayer be counted as incense before you, and the lifting up of my hands as the evening sacrifice!
—Psalm 141:2

Jane's prayer also teaches us that prayer can revive our hearts; when we feel dry, tired, and uninspired, prayer fills us with new life and breath. As we pray, a great exchange occurs: We empty ourselves of all our burdens and receive a fresh filling of joy, hope, and faith.

## Invitation to Pray

Has your prayer life been "fervent" or flat lately? Do you want to revive it? In the Bible, we read that the prayers of the saints are precious to God. Revelation 5:8 describes "golden bowls full of incense, which are the prayers of the saints" in the throne room of heaven. When God's children pray, he listens. *That* is exciting.

It's common to pray more fervently when we're in trouble or distress and less passionately when life is peaceful. If you're in a stormy season, let that propel you into fervent and heartfelt prayer. If you're in a calmer season, take this opportunity to pray specifically "for all the Lord's people" (Ephesians 6:18 NIV). Ask the Holy Spirit to lead you and position your heart to pray with a sense of urgency.

### Let Us Pray

*Thank you, Father in heaven, that you listen when I pray. I ask you now to incline my heart in fervent prayer. Please revive my heart and give me a renewed passion for praying regularly for my own needs and for your people. I invite you to lead me now, Holy Spirit, in a time of extended prayer. I need your help in this area of my prayer life: [your specific needs]. In Jesus' name, Amen.*

The effectual fervent prayer
of a righteous man availeth much.
—James 5:16 KJV

# *Day 22*

## REDEEMING THE TIME

*Another day is now gone, & added to those, for which we were before accountable. Teach us Almighty Father, to consider this solemn Truth, as we should do, that we may feel the importance of every day, & every hour as it passes, & earnestly strive to make a better use of what Thy Goodness may yet bestow on us, than we have done of the Time past.*

Mrs. John Dashwood in *Sense and Sensibility* is perhaps the greediest and most self-centered character in Jane Austen's novels. When her father-in-law dies, leaving his fortune and estate to her husband, she manipulates her husband so thoroughly that instead of giving his stepsisters "a thousand pounds a-piece,"[1] he decides to give them no financial help whatsoever. When the funeral is over, she arrives at Norland, "without sending any notice of her intention to her mother-in-law," with her son and their servants.[2] She "install[s] herself mistress," while "her mother and sisters-in-law" are "degraded to the condition of visitors."[3] Her only regret: that her mother-in-law gets to keep the "china, plate, and linen."[4]

Mrs. John Dashwood spends her days and time striving for one thing: more. Her life is focused solely on the accumulation of money and material goods. Though she has more than enough, she is not satisfied. She claims she wants her son, her husband, her brother, and even her mother to have more—but what she really wants is more for herself.

Now if anyone builds on the foundation with gold, silver, precious stones, wood, hay, straw—each one's work will become manifest, for the Day will disclose it.
—1 Corinthians 3:12–13

In contrast, Jane's prayer reveals that each day is a gift, meant to be spent with intention and purpose. In these lines, she prays for the ability to "feel the importance of every day, & every hour as it passes." Jane's words remind us that we are accountable to God for how we spend our days. She desires to "earnestly strive to make a better use" of each day.

We have the choice to invest our time, talent, and treasure in eternal things that will not pass away or in temporal things that will. In Matthew 6:19–20, Jesus says, "Do not lay up for yourselves treasures on earth, where moth and rust destroy and where thieves break in and steal, but lay up for yourselves treasures in heaven, where neither moth nor rust destroys and where thieves do not break in and steal." The lesson: Spiritual wealth is far better than worldly goods.

The desire for more is subtle and comes in many forms. However, focusing our time and energy on earthly goods and personal comforts only traps us in an unending loop. Beautiful homes become outdated and new cars get scratched. Health fails, natural disasters occur, world economies shift, and stock markets crash. When we trust anything to save us, secure us, or comfort us other than Christ, we build with faulty materials. Furthermore, we start to believe the lie that life on earth can or should be like heaven.

However, Jane's prayer reminds us that our time here on earth is finite and precious; we are "accountable" for each day. Making "better use" of our time doesn't necessarily mean working harder, multitasking, serving more, or accomplishing a list of tasks each day. It means living our lives *unto* God, investing in spiritual treasure, and "redeeming the time" (Ephesians 5:16 kjv).

> The kingdom of heaven is like treasure hidden in a field, which a man found and covered up. Then in his joy he goes and sells all that he has and buys that field.
> —Matthew 13:44

### Invitation to Pray

Do you want to build your life on a foundation of "gold, silver, precious stones" and "lay up treasure in heaven?" The primary way you can do this is by investing in your relationship with God and in helping others to know him more.

God's Word also teaches us to be mindful of how we spend our time. When you're standing in line at the store, you can pray for or talk to the people around you rather than check your phone. While you're driving, you can turn on worship music or a Bible teaching. When you're doing chores, you can pray and sing. During this time of prayer, ask the Lord to show you specific ways to invest in eternal things.

### Let Us Pray

*Thank you, Father, for this reminder that each day is a gift from you. I ask you now to show me how to spend my day. Please show me any activities I can trade for something far greater. I want to invest in my relationship with you, in the lives of others, and in eternal riches. I confess to you now my tendency to spend my time and energy on other things: [your specific tendencies]. In Jesus' name, Amen.*

Look carefully then how you walk,
not as unwise but as wise, making the best use
of the time, because the days are evil.
—Ephesians 5:15–16

# *Day 23*

## MAKE US LIKE YOU

*Give us Grace to endeavour after a truly Christian Spirit to seek to attain that temper of Forbearance & Patience, of which our Blessed Saviour has set us the highest Example, and which, while it prepares us for the spiritual Happiness of the life to come, will secure to us the best enjoyment of what this world can give.*

In this portion of her prayer, Jane prays for "a truly Christian Spirit." That spirit is one that looks like Jesus, our "highest Example." She prays for that "temper of Forbearance & Patience" that Jesus exemplified in his life and death. The reason: to prepare "for the spiritual Happiness of the life to come" and "secure . . . the best enjoyment of what this world can give."

Some of Jane Austen's more lively characters reveal the dangers associated with impatience and lack of self-control. Marianne Dashwood certainly doesn't believe in holding back; she lives for the thrill of human emotion. Lydia Bennet doesn't wait for excitement to find her but runs toward it, full-speed, come what may. Willoughby and Wickham each take what they want, when they want it, leaving a path of destruction in their wake.

In contrast, Jane's prayer reveals her desire to "attain that temper of Forbearance and Patience" that Jesus embodied. Another word for *forbearance* is "self-restraint";[1] the word *patience* in the New Testament means "to be long-spirited."[2] Jane asks God to infuse Christ's temperament into her own, asking for God's grace to "endeavour" to be more like him.

A man without self-control is like a city broken into and left without walls.
—Proverbs 25:28

Jane Bennet's self-control stands out in the Bennet household. She suffers silently in the face of disappointment and heartache, bears with her silly younger sisters, and deals kindly with her ill-tempered and bossy mother. And when the man she loves is whisked away by people determined to keep him from her, she settles her heart and tries "to get the better" of it.[3] Jane is a picture of calm patience in a house swirling with emotional upheaval:

> As for Jane, her anxiety under this suspense was, of course, more painful than Elizabeth's, but whatever she felt she was desirous of concealing, and between herself and Elizabeth, therefore, the subject was never alluded to. But as no such delicacy restrained her mother, an hour seldom passed in which she did not talk of

Bingley, express her impatience for his arrival, or even require Jane to confess that if he did not come back she would think herself very ill used. It needed all Jane's steady mildness to bear these attacks with tolerable tranquillity.[4]

Jane Bennet's "steady mildness" isn't due to a lack of feeling or emotion. In fact, she wishes her mother had "more command over herself" and says Mrs. Bennet "can have no idea of the pain she gives" by continually talking about Mr. Bingley.[5] However, she *chooses* self-control.

> Looking unto Jesus the author and finisher of our faith; who for the joy that was set before him endured the cross, despising the shame, and is set down at the right hand of the throne of God.
>
> —Hebrews 12:2 KJV

As Jane's prayer reminds us, forbearance and patience don't come naturally to most of us. We need God's grace to "attain" a temperament more like that of Jesus, our best and "highest Example." Jesus showed restraint in the most trying circumstances, even calmly and steadfastly setting his face toward Jerusalem and the cross that awaited him (Luke 9:51).

### Invitation to Pray

Do you become easily agitated or impatient? Do you tend to rush ahead, try to make things happen, or respond out of emotion? Most of us often find ourselves *causing* storms rather than *calming* them, especially when things feel out of control.

Jesus invites you to come to him. In Matthew 11:29, he says, "Take my yoke upon you, and learn from me, for I am gentle and lowly in heart, and you will find rest for your souls." Take this time to "learn" of Jesus and ask him to make you more like him.

### Let Us Pray

*Thank you, Jesus, for your patient, steadfast love for me. I want to be more like you and live a life of self-control and patience. When the storms hit, I tend to react based on emotion. I'm too quick to speak, I'm easily agitated, and I'm impatient. I ask you now to please speak into my heart and strengthen me to think and act more like you in this area of my life: [your specific needs]. In Jesus' name, Amen.*

Walk in a manner worthy of the calling to which you have been called, with all humility and gentleness, with patience, bearing with one another in love, eager to maintain the unity of the Spirit in the bond of peace.

—Ephesians 4:1–3

# Day 24

## SEARCH OUR HEARTS, O GOD

*Incline us Oh God! to think humbly of ourselves, to be severe
only in the examination of our own conduct, to consider our
fellow-creatures with kindness, & to judge of all they say & do
with that Charity which we would desire from Men ourselves.*

In *Mansfield Park*, Fanny Price struggles with less than charitable feelings toward Mary Crawford throughout the novel because she is jealous of the time and attention Edmund gives her. As Edmund becomes increasingly interested in Miss Crawford, Fanny is frequently displaced and forgotten: When Miss Crawford needs a horse to ride, she's given Fanny's mare; when Miss Crawford wants to walk farther at Sotherton, Fanny is left behind on a bench; and when Miss Crawford goes to the piano to sing, Edmund leaves Fanny's side to follow.

It's after Fanny sees Edmund and Miss Crawford riding together that she admits to herself that "she had been feeling neglected, and been struggling against discontent and envy for some days past."[1] Her feelings of "jealousy and agitation"[2] continue for most of the novel, and although Miss Crawford's manners and ideas are far different from her own, Fanny is perhaps more "severe" in her "examination" of Miss Crawford than she necessarily deserves.

In this portion of her prayer, Jane prays, "Incline us Oh God! to think humbly of ourselves, to be severe only in the examination of our own conduct." She desires to "consider" others with "kindness" and "judge" others with "Charity." Her words express a desire to extend grace to others and treat people the way she wishes to be treated.

Do nothing from selfish ambition or conceit, but in humility count others more significant than yourselves. Let each of you look not only to his own interests, but also to the interests of others.
—Philippians 2:3–4

Jane's prayer points us first to the cross. Paul writes that Jesus, "though he was in the form of God, did not count *equality with God* a thing to be grasped"; instead, he "emptied himself, by *taking the form of a servant*," and "*humbled himself* by becoming obedient to the point of death" (Philippians 2:6–8, emphasis mine). Jesus is our ultimate example of humility.

Jane's prayer also speaks to our attitudes toward and interactions with other people. Jane asks for God's help to be severe "only in the examination of our own conduct" and to "judge" what others "say & do with that Charity which we would desire from Men ourselves." This means giving people the benefit of the doubt and treating them the way we want to be treated.

Jane prays here for a paradigm shift that can only occur by the power of the Holy Spirit. The act of judging others based on how we want to be judged is the exact opposite of the world's expectations and our natural inclination. It's doing unto others as we would have them do unto us (Luke 6:31). We often judge others based on what they say or do or even by the expression on their face. However, such judgments are superficial and may be uncharitable; we cannot begin to know another person's true intentions and motives.

> Judge not, that you be not judged. For with the judgment you pronounce you will be judged, and with the measure you use it will be measured to you.
> —Matthew 7:1–2

### Invitation to Pray

Have you been slighted or hurt by something someone said or did? Sometimes it's hard to let things go, especially when people hurt our pride. Take this time now to ask God to show you if that person truly hurt you or merely bruised your pride. When our pride is injured, it's important to humble ourselves, let go of our hurt feelings, and give the other person the same grace we ourselves desire.

Deeper wounds are more difficult to process. Perhaps you're in need of a special touch from God because someone has hurt you intentionally, repeatedly, or in a serious way. May today be the day you open the door for God to come in and begin a work of healing and forgiveness in your heart. You can start by praying, "Lord, soften my heart."

### Let Us Pray

*Thank you, Jesus, for giving your life for mine. I want to treat others with humility and kindness. Please help me to love people the way I want to be loved. For my deepest wounds, I ask you now to heal my heart. In the area where my pride is injured, I lay it at your feet. Help me to forgive and seek unity above all else. I lift up to you now the wound that is hardest to forgive: [your specific needs]. In Jesus' name, Amen.*

Search me, O God, and know my heart!
Try me and know my thoughts! And see
if there be any grievous way in me,
and lead me in the way everlasting!
—Psalm 139:23–24

# *Day 25*

## INEXPRESSIBLE JOY

*We thank thee with all our hearts for every gracious dispensa-
tion, for all the Blessings that have attended our Lives, for every
hour of safety, health & peace, of domestic comfort & innocent
enjoyment.*

Jane once wrote in a letter to Cassandra, "I had a very pleasant
evening, however, though you will probably find out that there
was no particular reason for it; but I do not think it worth while
to wait for enjoyment until there is some real opportunity for it."[1]
On another occasion, she wrote this in her typical dry humor:
"Next week [I] shall begin my operations on my hat, on which
You know my principal hopes of happiness depend."[2]

Jane's words are witty and light-hearted. She seems to have
found pleasure in "domestic comfort & innocent enjoyment." She
was curious by nature and could amuse herself in an ordinary
gathering of people or in the basic trimming of a hat. She didn't

require new dresses, bright society, or unique experiences to enjoy life. Rather, it seems, she had a good time even when there "was no particular reason for it."[3]

In this portion of her prayer, Jane thanks God "for all the Blessings" that attend her and for "every hour of safety, health & peace." She recognizes that God's "gracious dispensation" is the true source of all "domestic comfort & innocent enjoyment" in life. From this prayer, it's clear that Jane was more than just happy about life. She had something even better: She had joy.

> Enter his gates with thanksgiving, and his courts with praise! Give thanks to him; bless his name!
> —Psalm 100:4

Where does one find joy? Many people in this world are looking for fulfillment, longing for happiness, and searching for a way to lift their spirits. People invest in gadgets and supplements, go long distances and travel to exotic destinations, and even delve into some rather strange practices—all to find a sense of bliss. But most of these things only provide periods of well-being. In the everyday, humdrum activities of life, where did Jane find her joy?

First Peter 1:8–9 (NIV) says, "Though you have not seen him, you love him; and even though you do not see him now, you believe in him and are filled with an inexpressible and glorious joy, for you are receiving the end result of your faith, the salvation of your souls." Could it be, then, that Jane had an invisible source of joy that came from the "end result" of her faith, in the "salvation of [her] soul"? Though Jane obviously faced trials and grief, we see evidence in her life that she was a woman "filled" with joy—in her writing, in her letters, and in her prayers.

The kind of joy that Peter references is not a feeling; rather, it is a result—the result of faith in Christ. It has nothing to do with circumstances, it's not something that you can find or conjure up, and it's not found in a pill or in an accomplishment. Joy isn't even the result of good things happening to us. In fact, the Bible says, "The joy of the Lord is your strength" in times of difficulty and sorrow (Nehemiah 8:10 NIV). Joy is not a state of *being*; it is a state of *believing*.

> Oh give thanks to the Lord, for he is good; for his steadfast love endures forever!
> —1 Chronicles 16:34

### Invitation to Pray

Do you struggle to find innocent enjoyment in life at times? Not every moment in life is comfortable or happy. In fact, many days are tiring, difficult, or even disappointing, and it's easy to become discouraged. Therefore, it's important to preach to our own hearts about the goodness and faithfulness of God. Psalm 42:5 shows us what to pray when we're troubled: "Why, my soul, are you downcast? Why so disturbed within me? Put your hope in God, for I will yet praise him, my Savior and my God" (NIV).

In addition to preaching good news to your own soul, it's important to ask God to encourage your heart as well. When you place your hope in God, your joy returns and your head lifts. Take this time now to ask God to renew a sense of hope in your heart.

### Let Us Pray

*Heavenly Father, thank you for your grace in my life and the blessing of belonging to you. Thank you for the many comforts you've given and how you provide even in the hard moments. In the areas where I'm uncomfortable, pinched, or unhappy, please open my eyes to the innocent enjoyments you provide. Please shine the light of your Word and your truth into the area where I'm most discouraged: [your specific needs]. In Jesus' name, Amen.*

Let them thank the Lord for his steadfast love,
for his wondrous works to the children of man!
And let them offer sacrifices of thanksgiving,
and tell of his deeds in songs of joy!
—Psalm 107:21–22

# Day 26

## BLESSED BEYOND DESERVING

*We feel that we have been blessed far beyond any thing that we have deserved; and though we cannot but pray for a continuance of all these Mercies, we acknowledge our unworthiness of them and implore Thee to pardon the presumption of our desires.*

Austen's novels are littered with characters who perhaps end up with better than they deserve. Edmund, after following Miss Crawford around like a lovesick puppy and giving up ground on many moral issues, still ends up with kind Fanny; Emma is forgiven her many failings and faults and marries generous Mr. Knightley; and Edward Ferrars, after making a foolish secret engagement with Lucy Steele, marries sensible Elinor. Grace is given and lessons are learned.

In Mrs. Bennet's case—even though she has zero discernment in choosing suitable marriage partners, is terribly vulgar, and gives only bad advice—she somehow ends up with her two eldest daughters married to kind, handsome men of good character, rank, and wealth. Though her parenting merits sons-in-law that more closely resemble Lydia's Mr. Wickham, Mrs. Bennet gets everything she wants: At the end of *Pride and Prejudice*, she is happy and secure.

Though Mrs. Bennet never fully realizes the extent of her own good luck, Jane recognizes that she and her family have been "blessed far beyond any thing that [they] have deserved." In this portion of her prayer, she asks God for a "continuance" of his mercies toward them, acknowledging that they are unworthy of so much. Her words are reminiscent of Psalm 103:10, which says God "does not treat us as our sins deserve or repay us according to our iniquities" (NIV).

> God shows his love for us in that while we were still sinners, Christ died for us.
> —Romans 5:8

Mrs. Bennet's problem is two-fold: She's dissatisfied with her current situation and worried about her future. She's done nothing to deserve the life she has, and yet she is unhappy. She lives in a comfortable home, has five daughters, plenty of friends, and dines with "four and twenty families,"[1] but it's not enough. As long as she thinks she *might* someday have to live on a small income with five daughters, that none of her five girls will ever marry, and that her husband may die before she does, she's insufferable.

Mrs. Bennet isn't happy until everything is perfectly settled in her world. This is a trap we all can easily fall into: Instead of enjoying the glorious riches of today, we spend our time looking forward to a bright someday yet to come, worrying about the future, and planning for the what-ifs. We spend our lives working toward the day when everything will finally fall into place. Meanwhile, *we're* insufferable.

In Jane's prayer, she prays "for a continuance of all these Mercies," asking for God's provision and protection; however, her words also express an underlying sense of contentment. As children of God, we've already been "blessed far beyond any thing that we have deserved." Our inheritance, our reward, is kept for us in heaven. Until then, we can trust God's plans, provision, and purposes for our days here on earth.

Now to him who is able to do far more abundantly than all that we ask or think, according to the power at work within us, to him be glory in the church and in Christ Jesus throughout all generations, forever and ever.
—Ephesians 3:20–21

### Invitation to Pray

When you face uncertainties about your future, health, or finances, do you become unsettled and fretful? Do you look forward to the day when you've finally paid your dues and can relax and enjoy life? Be encouraged! God has a work for you to do right now and in the future, no matter your age, abilities, or circumstances.

Jesus did not die and redeem us, body, soul, and spirit, so we could live out our days in perpetual vacation mode. Instead, we are called to serve and love Jesus, care for others, and help people know him. When we seek first his kingdom and his righteousness, God supplies the rest (Matthew 6:33). Take this time to reflect on all you've been given and seek his face for today.

### Let Us Pray

*Thank you, Lord, for this reminder of the many gifts and comforts you've given to me. I want to live my life today for you, not for the perfect someday in my imagination. I want to seek first your kingdom and your righteousness and be used for your good purposes. Please speak to my heart about the situations and circumstances that cause me to feel unsettled and unsatisfied: [your specific needs]. In Jesus' name, Amen.*

Therefore I tell you, do not be anxious about your life, what you will eat, nor about your body, what you will put on. For life is more than food, and the body more than clothing.

Luke 12:22–23

## Day 27

# MORNING DAWNS AND
# EVENING FADES

*Keep us Oh! Heavenly Father from Evil this night. Bring us in*
*safety to the beginning of another day & grant that we may rise*
*again with every serious & religious feeling which now directs us.*

Jane experienced a season in her life that was marked by loss
and change. In 1797, Cassandra's fiancé died in the West In-
dies. In 1801, Jane's father retired and moved their family to Bath,
away from her beloved Hampshire. Then in 1806, while in Bath,
her dear father died suddenly and without warning. Jane didn't
write as much during her years in Bath, which some attribute
to a lack of inspiration or a dislike of the town itself. However,
it may be that Jane was affected most by who and what she lost
while living there.

Jane felt "happy feelings of Escape" when they left Bath for Clifton.[1] Indeed, it must have been a relief to escape the painful memories associated with Bath. When Edward later offered her mother a small house on his Chawton estate, life brightened for Jane. They settled in Hampshire, amongst family and friends, and Jane began writing again. After a period of darkness, light dawned once more for Jane.

> Weeping may
> endure for a night,
> but joy comes in
> the morning.
> —Psalm 30:5, NKJV

In this portion of Jane's prayer, she prays against the evils of "this night," asking God to bring them "in safety to the beginning of another day." Though Jane prays for their actual physical safety, her prayer also echoes many Bible verses that speak of morning and evening as more than just times of day. The night often represents times of spiritual darkness, endings, grief, and difficulty. Morning speaks of new life, new mercies, new beginnings, and new hope.

Some seasons in life are fraught with trial and difficulty. We experience painful losses that bring with them the need for deep healing and great measures of comfort. And just when it seems as though the darkness of pain and loss will never cease, God brings the morning. He lightens the load of sorrow and carries us through to safety. As we seek his face, he brings the dawn of healing.

Many of the Psalms speak of God's help, renewal, and revival coming in the morning. Psalm 90:14 says, "Satisfy us in the morning with your steadfast love, that we may rejoice and be glad all our days." Psalm 46:5 says, "God is in the midst of her; she shall not be moved; God will help her when morning dawns." And Psalm 59:16 says, "I will sing aloud of your steadfast love in the morning. For you have been to me a fortress and a refuge in the day of my distress."

Jane came through her evening of sorrow and made a fresh start at Chawton. She poured her love and attention into her family and friends, nieces and nephews. She pulled out and revised old drafts of her early works and drafted new novels. She found fresh inspiration and began to write at a pace and level unlike ever before. During this time of renewal, Jane discovered that writing wasn't just an entertaining pastime—it was her life's calling. As she started over in Hampshire, a new passion and purpose was born.

The steadfast love of the Lord never ceases; his mercies never come to an end; they are new every morning; great is your faithfulness.
—Lamentations 3:22–23

## Invitation to Pray

Are you waiting for morning to dawn after a long night of difficulty, sorrow, or mourning? There are times when the ache of loss is so great, all we can do is sit on the train of Jesus' robe and weep. God's Word says, "'For I know the plans I have for you,' declares the Lord, 'plans to prosper you and not to harm you, plans to give you hope and a future'" (Jeremiah 29:11 NIV).

God gives us new opportunities each day to "rise again with every serious & religious feeling which now directs us." As we seek God's face, immerse ourselves in his Word, and pray at his feet, healing comes. Gentle showers come to refresh us. The sun breaks over the tops of the mountains. God's tender mercies come, and we begin again.

### Let Us Pray

*Heavenly Father, thank you for this timely reminder of your plans for my life and for renewal, healing, and new beginnings. I come to you now, my heart in my hands, asking you to shed your light on the dark places of my life. I need your touch of comfort and healing. I ask you to please bring the morning light, a new dawn, to the part of my life that has felt like the night: [your specific needs]. In Jesus' name, Amen.*

Let the morning bring me word of your
unfailing love, for I have put my trust in you.
Show me the way I should go,
for to you I entrust my life.
—Psalm 143:8, NIV

# Day 28

## GO INTO THE WORLD

*May thy mercy be extended over all Mankind, bringing the Igno-
rant to the knowledge of thy Truth, awakening the Impenitent,
touching the Hardened.*

In *Jane Austen: The Parson's Daughter,* Irene Collins says Jane
was "encouraged to strengthen her faith by prayer and worship, but to make her witness in the world through her behavior
to others rather than by preaching."[1] Though Jane's father and
brothers did preach from a pulpit, she herself preached a more
subtle sermon in the way she lived and wrote.

In her novels, there is one character in particular who experi-
ences personal awakening: Tom Bertram in *Mansfield Park.* Simi-
lar to the prodigal son in the Bible, Tom's "extravagance" is great.
He spends his own inheritance and robs his younger brother
Edmund "of more than half the income which ought to be his."[2]
Tom's lifestyle finally catches up to him when he goes "with a party

of young men to Newmarket." There, "a neglected fall and a good deal of drinking" bring on a fever. His friends leave him behind in "sickness and solitude."[3]

In this line of her prayer, Jane expresses a desire to see "all Mankind" come into the "knowledge" of God's "Truth." This evange-listic prayer focuses on the redemption of the world. In John 14:6, Jesus says there is one way to know God: "I am the way, and the truth, and the life. No one comes to the Father except through me." Jane prays for an "awak-ening" for "the Impenitent" and asks God to touch "the Hardened."

Today, if you hear his voice, do not harden your hearts as in the rebellion.
—Hebrews 3:15

In Tom's case, his need for peni-tence and awakening is clear. When Tom is all alone and "dangerously ill," Edmund goes to "attend him."[4] Tom experiences ups and downs in his recovery, but when the news of his sister's elopement comes, his "complaints" are "greatly heightened" and "his recovery [is] much thrown back."[5] Tom finally becomes so ill his family fears for his safety.

When Tom does eventually recover, he is a changed man. We read that he "regained his health, without regaining the thought-lessness and selfishness of his previous habits. He was the better for ever for his illness. He had suffered, and he had learned to think."[6] Tom's illness makes "an impression on his mind" that is "durable in its happy effects."[7] His hardened heart is softened permanently, and he experiences a powerful awakening from his reflections while he is sick. In the end, Tom becomes "what he ought to be: useful to his father, steady and quiet, and not living merely for himself."[8]

Jane's prayer focuses on this kind of awakening and echoes the Great Commission Jesus gives his followers in Matthew 28:19–20: "Go therefore and make disciples of all nations, baptizing them in the name of the Father and of the Son and of the Holy Spirit, teaching them to observe all that I have commanded you." Though Jane never preached a sermon and rarely moralized in her novels, her life and prayers reveal her desire to know God more and see others come to know him as well.

> In the same way, let your light shine before others, so that they may see your good works and give glory to your Father who is in heaven.
> —Matthew 5:16

### Invitation to Pray

You, too, preach a sermon with your life. What you do with your time, talent, and treasure says a lot about you. The things that make you angry and the things you work the hardest to get reveal what you value most. What values are you preaching to your family, friends, children, and colleagues? During this time of reflection, think about what you want to preach with your life.

Or perhaps you have a "Tom" in your life. Someone who lives for entertainment and empty amusement or has been hardened by life, sin, addiction, disappointment, loss, or abuse. Who do you know that needs spiritual revival and awakening and an intimate knowledge of Christ? Take this time now to ask the Holy Spirit to rouse the impenitent and touch the hardened.

### Let Us Pray

*Jesus, thank you for your promise that anyone who believes in you will not perish but have eternal life (John 3:16). Please show me what sermon I'm preaching to the people around me and what I'm worshiping with my time, talent, and treasure. I want my life to be an illustration of your redeeming power and love. Please use me to shine your light into the life of that hardened person in my life: [specific name(s) here]. In Jesus' name, Amen.*

Just so, I tell you, there will be more joy
in heaven over one sinner who repents
than over ninety-nine righteous persons
who need no repentance.

—Luke 15:7

# Day 29

## LOOK WITH COMPASSION

*Look with compassion upon the afflicted of every condition, as-*
*suage the pangs of disease, comfort the broken in spirit.*

In this portion of her prayer, Jane asks God to "look with compassion" on those who are "afflicted," experiencing the "pangs
of disease," or who are "broken in spirit." In Jane's novels, when
someone is ill or distressed, their friends and family provide tangible help and comfort. In the same way, Jane and Cassandra
frequently nursed family members when they were ill.

When their brother Henry became suddenly and severely ill
during one of Jane's visits to him in London, Caroline Austen said,
"Aunt Cass. stayed on nearly a month, and Aunt Jane remained
some weeks longer, to nurse the convalescent."[1] When Jane herself
fell ill during the last year of her life, Cassandra accompanied her
to Winchester for medical care and stayed by her side. Caroline's
mother ( Jane's lifelong friend Mrs. Mary Austen, née Lloyd) went

as well, both "to make it more cheerful for them" and to "take a share in the necessary attendance."[2] Jane was never alone: "Aunt Cassandra and my Mother and my Aunt's maid took the nights between them."[3]

The child of God is also never alone. In this portion of her prayer, Jane asks God to "look with compassion upon the afflicted of every condition, assuage the pangs of disease, comfort the broken in spirit." This points to the unique care God gives to his people, to his tangible presence, and to the comfort he gives to those in pain.

> Let your steadfast love comfort me according to your promise to your servant.
>
> —Psalm 119:76

Cassandra sat with Jane day by day, hour by hour, during her decline in health. After Jane passed away, Cassandra wrote to their niece Fanny Knight: "I thank God that I was enabled to attend her to the last."[4] Cassandra sat with her, read to her, and prayed for her.[5] Surely, Cassandra drew comfort from being able to care for Jane during those difficult and precious final hours. She said, "I was able to close her eyes myself, and it was a great gratification to me to render her those last services."[6]

Jane's prayer reminds us that God is our ultimate source of "compassion" and "comfort" in times of distress or illness. In those final days, Jane and Cassandra also must have drawn strength from their faith in God's character and promises. In Cassandra's letter to Fanny she writes these words: "I likewise know that you will apply to the fountain-head for consolation, and that our merciful God is never deaf to such prayers as you will offer."[7] And in another letter: "I hope I am properly grateful to the Almighty for having been so supported."[8] Cassandra cared for Jane and then released her into God's ultimate care and keeping.

The Psalms remind us over and over again that God's "steadfast love" comforts us "according to" his "promise" (Psalm 119:76). Psalm 34:18 tells us, "The Lord is near to the brokenhearted and saves the crushed in spirit." Psalm 55:22 gives this promise: "Cast your burden on the Lord, and he will sustain you; he will never permit the righteous to be moved."

Remember your word to your servant, in which you have made me hope. This is my comfort in my affliction, that your promise gives me life.
—Psalm 119:49–50

### Invitation to Pray

Are you feeling lost, broken, or crushed in spirit? Or do you know someone in that state? Humans can go without food for several weeks, without water for several days, and without air for several minutes, but it's been said that people can't survive even a few moments without hope. In the midst of difficulty and trial, being "broken in spirit" is one of the most difficult afflictions to endure: "A man's spirit will endure sickness, but a crushed spirit who can bear?" (Proverbs 18:14).

In the last part of her prayer, Jane asks God to shine a light into the lives of people who have no hope. This is a wonderful prayer to pray for someone who is discouraged. Take this time now to pray for the reality of Christ's love to come down in showers of hope today.

### Let Us Pray

*Dear heavenly Father, thank you that I can turn to you for comfort and help. I bring before you the people I know who are sick, in trouble, or who have a crushed, hopeless spirit: [specific names here]. Show me how to comfort and care for them with your love. Give me your words to encourage them. Stir up hope in my heart today in the area where I need it most: [your specific needs]. In Jesus' name, Amen.*

I would have despaired unless I had believed
that I would see the goodness of the Lord
in the land of the living. Wait for the Lord;
be strong and let your heart take courage;
yes, wait for the Lord.
—Psalm 27:13–14 NASB

# Day 30

## THY HEAVENLY KINGDOM

*More particularly do we pray for the safety and welfare of our own family & friends wheresoever dispersed, beseeching Thee to avert from them all material & lasting Evil of Body or Mind; & may we by the assistance of thy Holy Spirit so conduct ourselves on Earth as to secure an Eternity of Happiness with each other in thy Heavenly Kingdom.*

In this portion of her prayer, Jane prays for the "safety and welfare" of her family and friends, asking God to keep them from "all material & lasting Evil of Body or Mind." She also asks for the "assistance of [God's] Holy Spirit" to conduct herself on earth and looks forward to "an Eternity of Happiness" with her family in God's "Heavenly Kingdom."

Jane grew up praying with her family, reading the Bible, and attending church. She knew about life and death, and because of her faith in Christ, she believed this earth was not her final home:

"But our citizenship is in heaven, and from it we await a Savior, the Lord Jesus Christ, who will transform our lowly body to be like his glorious body, by the power that enables him even to subject all things to himself" (Philippians 3:20–21).

Jane's prayer also reveals that she looked forward to her eternal home. In John 14, Jesus says this about heaven: "In my Father's house are many rooms. If it were not so, would I have told you that I go to prepare a place for you? And if I go and prepare a place for you, I will come again and will take you to myself, that where I am you may be also" (vv. 2–3).

> For he was looking forward to the city that has foundations, whose designer and builder is God.
> —Hebrews 11:10

Regarding Jane's illness, her niece Caroline writes that Jane was "quite aware of her own danger" and yet was peaceful and composed:

She was a humble and beleiving [sic] Christian; her life had passed in the cheerful performance of all home duties, and with no aiming at applause, she had sought, as if by instinct to promote the happiness of all those who came within her influence—doubtless she had her reward, in the peace of mind which was granted to her in her last days.[1]

Jane professed faith in Christ and put her trust in God's Word. Jane cherished her life and her family here on earth, but she also had the hope of heaven to sustain her.

In her letters to Fanny Knight, Cassandra refers to "a far superior Mansion" and being "reunited" with Jane one day.[2] She writes, "May the sorrow with which she is parted with on earth be a prognostic of the joy with which she is hailed in Heaven!"[3] The apostle Paul wrote this: "But we do not want you to be uninformed, brothers, about those who are asleep, that you may not grieve as others do who have no hope. For since we believe that Jesus died and rose again, even so, through Jesus, God will bring with him those who have fallen asleep" (1 Thessalonians 4:13–14).

When we read what the Bible has to say about eternal life with God, death loses its sting (1 Corinthians 15:55). Jane's prayer reminds us that she looked forward to that "Heavenly Kingdom," where there will be no more tears, no more sorrow, no more illness (Revelation 21:4). Her belief in "an Eternity of Happiness with each other" gave her hope.

> You make known to
> me the path of life;
> in your presence there
> is fullness of joy;
> at your right hand are
> pleasures forevermore.
> —Psalm 16:11

## Invitation to Pray

Have you suffered the loss of a loved one or friend? This side of heaven, losing someone dear is heartbreaking. We miss them terribly and feel as though something is missing in our lives. The sense of loss is often painful and overwhelming. Truly, the only hope we have in the face of death is the hope of heaven.

Do you wonder what happens after this life? God does not want you to live in fear or in hopelessness. Take time to look up today's Scripture verses about heaven in your Bible. If you want to know about how to become a Christian and have eternal life, please turn to the Special Invitation section at the end of this devotional on page 146.

### *Let Us Pray*

*Thank you, Lord, for showing me that there is hope in this life and beyond. I want to know you more and know what the Bible says about heaven, so I don't have to be afraid. Please lead me and guide me to learn about your great promises, so I can encourage others to know you and trust you. Please help me in the area where I am most fearful and unsure: [your specific needs]. In Jesus' name, Amen.*

[God] will wipe away every tear from
their eyes, and death shall be no more,
neither shall there be mourning, nor crying,
nor pain anymore, for the former
things have passed away.
—Revelation 21:4

# *Day 31*

## OUR FATHER

*Hear us Almighty God, for His sake who has redeemed us, &*
*taught us thus to pray.*

*Pardon Oh Lord! the imperfections of these our Prayers, &*
*accept them through the mediation of our Blessed Saviour, in*
*whose Holy Words, we further address thee.*

*Grant this most merciful Father, for the sake of our Blessed*
*Saviour in whose Holy Name & Words we further address Thee.*

These are the closing lines from each of Jane's three prayers.
With these words, Jane concludes her own prayers and
leads into the Lord's Prayer, which would have most likely been
recited out loud, corporately. In these lines, Jane asks their "Almighty God" and "most merciful Father" to hear their prayers,
"for His sake who has redeemed us," referring to their "Blessed
Saviour," Jesus Christ, saying that it's in his name and "Words"
that they pray.

Jane's reference to "the mediation of our blessed Saviour" is a wonderful reminder of who we are *in* Christ. The Bible says there is "one God and one mediator between God and mankind, the man Christ Jesus, who gave himself as a ransom for all people" (1 Timothy 2:5–6 NIV). Jesus is our redeemer, our "Blessed Saviour," through whom we have received forgiveness and the remission of sin. Jesus is the reason we have a place prepared for us in heaven and an inheritance waiting. He's the very reason we have access to God in prayer.

> Let us then approach God's throne of grace with confidence, so that we may receive mercy and find grace to help us in our time of need.
>
> —Hebrews 4:16 NIV

Romans 8:34 says, "Christ Jesus is the one who died—more than that, who was raised—who is at the right hand of God, who indeed is interceding for us." Jesus stands at the right hand of the Father, on our behalf, having justified us with his own blood, so that we can come to God's "throne of grace" with confidence in prayer.

Jesus, our mediator, also taught us *how* to pray. Each of Jane's prayers ends with the Lord's Prayer, the prayer Jesus gave his disciples in Matthew 6:9–13. Jane and her family all knew it by heart and recited it regularly as part of the liturgy of the Church of England:

Our Father which art in heaven, Hallowed be thy Name. Thy Kingdom come. Thy will be done in Earth, As it is in Heaven.

Give us this day our daily bread. And forgive us our trespasses,
As we forgive them, that trespass against us. And lead us not into
temptation; But deliver us from evil: For thine is the Kingdom,
the Power, And the Glory, For ever and ever. Amen.[1]

The Lord's Prayer gives us a model for prayer, reminding us of
the simple and essential components of prayer. When we pray it,
we proclaim our desire to honor him, see his kingdom come, and
see his will done. We ask for our daily bread—his provision for
our lives—both spiritually and physi-
cally. In it, we ask forgiveness of
our own sins, as we in turn forgive
others. We ask for the Lord's protection from temptation and evil.

> To you, O Lord,
> I lift up my soul.
> —Psalm 25:1

The Lord's Prayer speaks of a life
surrendered to God. Jane's prayers
echo many of the same concepts and
themes found in the Lord's Prayer, and she ends each of her
prayers with the words of Jesus, praying, "Our Father."

## Invitation to Pray

Jane's prayers reveal a life surrendered to God, a faith that
was vibrant and real. She prayed to her "Almighty Father" with
confidence in his fatherly goodness, kindness, and faithfulness.
She came to God's throne of grace in prayer, asking for his help,
provision, and protection in her life.

How have Jane's faith and prayers inspired you? Perhaps you've started to have a time of daily prayer or have begun to feel more confident praying on your own. Or perhaps you're reading your Bible more, wanting to know the God Jane knew and loved. Take this time to pray through the Lord's Prayer slowly, meditating on what it means to honor God with your life, look forward to his heavenly kingdom, and truly desire his will to be done in your life.

### Let Us Pray

*Heavenly Father, thank you that you hear me when I pray. I ask you to bring your kingdom into my life here on earth, as it is in heaven. Please grow my prayer life, help me continue in it, let me never grow weary or lax. I want to learn to pray like Jesus prayed and honor you in every part of my life. Please work and move in my heart today in this area: [your specific request]. In Jesus' name, Amen.*

The Lord is near to all who call on him,
to all who call on him in truth.
Psalm 145:18

# EPILOGUE

*A Lasting Legacy*

Jane left a rich legacy behind her as a beloved daughter, sister, friend, and aunt. In Cassandra's letter to Fanny Knight after Jane passed away, she wrote about what Jane meant to her:

> I have lost a treasure, such a sister, such a friend as never can have been surpassed. She was the sun of my life, the gilder of every pleasure, the soother of every sorrow; I had not a thought concealed from her, and it is as if I had lost a part of myself. I loved her only too well.[1]

Psalm 116:15 says, "Precious in the sight of the Lord is the death of his saints." This is surely true of Jane. Her tomb at Winchester Cathedral, close to where she lived on College Street during her final year, is inscribed with these beautiful words:

> In Memory of JANE AUSTEN [. . .] The benevolence of her heart, the sweetness of her temper, and the extraordinary endowments of

her mind obtained the regard of all who knew her and the warmest love of her intimate connections. Their grief is in proportion to their affection, they know their loss to be irreparable, but in their deepest affliction they are consoled by a firm though humble hope that her charity, devotion, faith and purity have rendered her soul acceptable in the sight of her REDEEMER.[2]

These words speak of a life well-lived and a loving circle of family and friends. Later, a plaque was added that speaks about her writing, the "varied charms of her character," and her "Christian faith and piety." It ends with this Bible verse: "She openeth her mouth with wisdom; and in her tongue is the law of kindness" (Proverbs 31:26 KJV).[3]

Reflecting on the prayers of a woman who became, posthumously, one of the most famous female authors in history is humbling and gratifying. She lived a relatively quiet life, in an obscure village in the south of England, but she had an extraordinary gift for writing. When she wrote during the day, she quickly hid her writing "with a piece of blotting paper"[4] whenever anyone other than immediate family came in. However, her gift could not, would not, be hidden. Her writing outlasts her now by over 200 years, and yet it remains as remarkable today as it was when it was first printed.

We too can live extraordinary lives. Though we may not ever be famous, we all leave behind us a legacy. We will be remembered for who we are more than for what we do. Our friends and family will speak of us based on what they saw of our lives, the way we treated people, and the way we loved. And, hopefully, like Jane, we will be best known for our faith in God, the way we love Jesus, and the way we serve him and teach others about him.

One generation shall commend
your works to another,
and shall declare your mighty acts.
—Psalm 145:4

# Special Invitation

Do you want to know the same "Almighty Father" Jane Austen knew and loved? Do you want to be set free from sin, forgiven, redeemed, and made new? Do you want to know Jesus as your personal Lord and Savior? You can do that, today.

The Bible says that every person sins and falls short of the glory of God (Romans 3:23). The penalty for sin is death (Romans 6:23). Apart from Jesus, we are spiritually dead in our trespasses and sin. We must be born again—spiritually reborn—or we won't see the kingdom of God (John 3:3). Jesus said there is only *one way* to know God: "I am *the* way, and *the* truth, and *the* life. No one comes to the Father *except through me*" (John 14:6; emphasis mine).

The Good News is this: Jesus made the ultimate sacrifice and paid the penalty for sin when he died on the cross. He gave his life as a ransom, to pay for our release from the bondage of sin and death. He died, was buried, and rose again the third day, victorious. Those who put their faith in Jesus as their Savior will not perish but have eternal life (John 3:16).

In Acts 16:31, the jailer asks Paul and Silas what he must do to be saved. They reply, "Believe in the Lord Jesus, and you will be saved."

Jesus says, "Behold, I stand at the door and knock. If anyone hears my voice and opens the door, I will come in to him and eat with him, and he with me" (Revelation 3:20). Jesus is knocking on the door of your heart today. Will you invite him in?

If you've never given your life to Christ, you can ask Jesus to be your personal Lord and Savior and start your new life with him right now. Or if you're that prodigal who's wandered away from the Lord, you can recommit your life to Christ. Don't delay; he welcomes you back with open arms. If you pray this prayer from your heart, God will hear and answer. Romans 10:13 says, "Everyone who calls on the name of the Lord will be saved."

> For the wages of sin is death, but the free gift of God is eternal life in Christ Jesus our Lord.
> —Romans 6:23

### Let Us Pray

*Lord Jesus, I confess to you that I'm a sinner. I believe you died on the cross and shed your blood for every sin I ever committed. I repent now of my sin and I ask you to forgive me. I choose to follow you from this moment forward as my Savior and Lord. Thank you for loving me, accepting me, and forgiving me. In Jesus' name I pray, Amen.*

### Next Steps

If you prayed that prayer, praise God! You are now a child of God. Be sure to tell someone this good news. It's important to believe in your heart *and* confess with your lips that you belong to Jesus (Romans 10:9). Connect with a local church as well, so you can grow in your relationship with Christ and with other Christians.

I invite you to connect with me as well at racheldodge.com. I would love to hear your story, answer any questions, and pray for you.

If you declare with your mouth, "Jesus is Lord," and believe in your heart that God raised him from the dead, you will be saved.

—Romans 10:9 NIV

# ACKNOWLEDGMENTS

It is a truth universally acknowledged, that a writer in possession of a good book idea must be in want of an agent. Thank you to Janet Grant of Books & Such Literary Management for giving me and my writing the opportunity to soar. Your time, patience, and wise counsel are a comfort and a gift. Thank you for taking me on and keeping me grounded!

Thank you to everyone at Bethany House who helped make this dream a reality. Thank you to Kim Bangs for taking a chance on a new author and to Ellen Chalifoux and Andy McGuire for seeing me through the editorial process. You each are a joy to work with, and I have a feeling you've spoiled me by giving me an incredible first experience publishing a book.

Thank you to David Bell for being a wonderfully picky first reader and advisor. I'm grateful for your knowledge and insight about all things Austen. Thank you for the many times you set aside other projects to look at this. Working together was a high-light in this process.

Thank you to "my dearest" Joanna Weaver—my mentor, encourager, and friend—for reminding me that God's plans are so much bigger and more exciting than we often dare to imagine.

Thank you to Victoire "Vic" Sanborn for bringing me on at *Jane Austen's World* and for generously sharing your knowledge about Jane Austen and the world of blogging.

Thank you to Wendy Lawton and Michelle Ule of Books & Such Literary Management for your help and wisdom on this journey.

Thank you to Janice Braun and the staff at the Elinor Raas Heller Rare Book Room at Mills College for your expertise and for letting me sit with Jane's prayers as long as I liked.

Thank you to "The Supper Club"—Robin Phillips, Shauna Pilgreen, and Mandy Santos—for your prayers and encouragement. I never cease to thank God for you; you are my secret weapon and kindred spirits.

Thank you to Maddy Swendner for being the one and only "Maddy!!" You are the original kid-whisperer and Maddy Express. Thank you for the countless times you stepped in to ease the load for me so I could write this book. I can't imagine our family without you in it!

Thank you to my dear friends and sisters in Christ for your steadfast love, encouragement, and prayers for me through this process: Courtney Boudreau, Meghan Clark, Leann Crutchfield, Carolyn Frank, Tammy Gurzhiy, Hennie McIntire, Kerry Morsey, Kristi Rapoza, and Jenice Williams. Thank you for battling in prayer for me as I wrote this book.

Thank you to Richard and Valerie Cimino for your love and support through the years. Richard, as my pastor and my Bible teacher, thank you for your faithful Bible teaching every Sunday and Monday, verse by verse, chapter by chapter, book by book. Valerie, thank you for your wisdom, prayers, and encouragement and for teaching me to *love* God's Word.

Thank you to my brother, Matthew Beckman—an amazing brother, friend, and writer—for inviting me to my first writers conference and for pressing me to "keep writing!" so many times. You have always been and continue to be my favorite collaborator.

Thank you to my parents, George and Ruth Beckman, for giving me the place and space to dream. Mom, you provided stacks of books, beautiful gardens, and bins full of play clothes so I could be whomever I wanted to be. Dad, you taught me to love words and classic literature and told me I was supposed to write books. Thank you for never giving up on me.

Thank you to my children, Lizzy and Jack, for being my biggest fans. Thank you for cheering for me and asking so many questions and for the many times you happily played in your imaginary world so I could write. You make my heart happy. I love you both!

Finally, thank you to my husband and best friend, Bobby. Thank you for loving and supporting me so selflessly, so that I can follow my dreams that have to do with all the words that mean so much to me but are a bit mysterious to you. You deserve a million hero points for watching *all* the movies, for trekking with me to "Austen-land," and for listening to me ramble about Jane Austen for nearly two decades now. Thank you, my love!

# NOTES

### Introduction

1. Bruce Stovel, "'A Nation Improving in Religion': Jane Austen's Prayers and Their Place in Her Life and Art," *Persuasions*, no. 16 (1994):185–196, www.jasna.org /persuasions/printed/number16/stovel.htm.

2. Laura Mooneyham White, *Jane Austen's Anglicanism* (London: Routledge Taylor & Francis Group, 2011), 5.

3. Irene Collins, *Jane Austen: The Parson's Daughter* (London: Bloomsbury, 1998), 72.

4. Jane Austen, *Jane Austen's Letters*, ed. Deirdre Le Faye, 4th ed. (Oxford: Oxford University Press, 2011), 157.

### Day 1  Give Us Grace, Almighty Father

1. William Austen-Leigh and Richard Arthur Austen-Leigh, *Jane Austen: Her Life and Letters, A Family Record (1913)*, (New York: Barnes & Noble, 2006), 17.

2. Austen-Leigh and Austen-Leigh, *Life and Letters*, 143.

3. Austen-Leigh and Austen-Leigh, *Life and Letters*, 144.

### Day 2  An Ever-Present Help

1. Austen-Leigh and Austen-Leigh, *Life and Letters*, 18.

2. Austen-Leigh and Austen-Leigh, *Life and Letters*, 20.

3. Austen-Leigh and Austen-Leigh, *Life and Letters*, 20.

### Day 3  Fix Our Thoughts

1. Jane Austen, *Persuasion*, ed. R. W. Chapman (Oxford: Oxford University Press, 1988), 237.

2. Austen, *Persuasion*, 232.

3. Austen, *Persuasion*, 237.

### Day 4  Give Us Pure Hearts

1. Jane Austen, *Emma*, ed. R. W. Chapman (Oxford: Oxford University Press, 1988), 370.

2. Austen, *Emma*, 375.

3. Austen, *Emma*, 375–6.

4. Austen, *Emma*, 376.

### Day 5  A Day Well Spent

1. Constance Hill, *Jane Austen: Her Homes & Her Friends (1901)*, (Dodo Press, 2008), 139.

### Day 6  Open Our Eyes

1. Jane Austen, *Pride and Prejudice*, ed. R. W. Chapman (Oxford: Oxford University Press, 1988), 208.

2. Austen, *Pride and Prejudice*, 76.

3. Austen, *Pride and Prejudice*, 76.

### Day 7  Every Good and Perfect Gift

1. James Edward Austen-Leigh, *Memoir of Jane Austen (1870)*. (CreateSpace Independent Publishing, 2014), chap. 2.

### Day 8  Under His Care

1. Jane Austen, *Sense and Sensibility*, ed. R. W. Chapman (Oxford: Oxford University Press, 1988), 307.

2. Austen, *Sense and Sensibility*, 310.

3. Austen, *Sense and Sensibility*, 310.

4. Austen, *Sense and Sensibility*, 315.

5. Austen, *Sense and Sensibility*, 315.

6. *Blue Letter Bible*, Strong's Definitions, s.v. "*fellowship*," www.blueletterbible.org/lang/lexicon/lexicon.cfm?Strongs=G2842&t=ESV.

## Day 9  Help for the Helpless

1. Austen, *Sense and Sensibility*, 23.

2. Maggie Lane, *Jane Austen's Family: Through Five Generations* (London: Robert Hale, 1984), 195.

## Day 10  A Genuine Faith

1. Jane Austen, *Mansfield Park*, ed. R. W. Chapman (Oxford: Oxford University Press, 1988), 7.

## Day 11  Look Down with Favor

1. Austen-Leigh, *Memoir*, chap. 2.

2. Deirdre Le Faye, *Jane Austen: The World of Her Novels* (London: Frances Lincoln, 2002), 13.

3. Collins, *Parson's Daughter*, 48.

## Day 12  Make Us Mindful

1. *The Book of Common Prayer: The Texts of 1549, 1559, and 1662*, ed. Brian Cummings (Oxford: Oxford University Press, 2013), 251.

## Day 13  Invade Our Habits

1. Caroline Austen, *My Aunt Jane: A Memoir (1867)*, (Winchester, UK: Sarsen Press, 1952), 6–7.

2. *Blue Letter Bible*, Strong's Definitions, s.v. "withdraw," www.blueletterbible.org/lang/lexicon/lexicon.cfm?Strongs=G5298&t=KJV.

## Day 14  Guard Our Hearts

1. Austen, *Sense and Sensibility*, 42.

2. Austen, *Sense and Sensibility*, 48.

3. Austen, *Sense and Sensibility*, 48.

4. Austen, *Sense and Sensibility*, 48.

## Day 15  A Good Father

1. Austen, *Letters*, 163.

2. Austen, *Letters*, 163–4.

## Day 16  A Benevolent Spirit

1. Austen-Leigh, *Memoir*, chap. 5.
2. Austen-Leigh, *Memoir*, chap. 5.
3. Austen-Leigh, *Memoir*, chap. 5.

## Day 17  Give Us Patience

1. Austen, *Mansfield Park*, 20.

## Day 18  Keep the Night Watches

1. Jane Austen, *Northanger Abbey*, ed. by R. W. Chapman (Oxford: Oxford University Press, 1988), 167.
2. Austen, *Northanger Abbey*, 170.

## Day 20  A Fervent Faith

1. Austen, *Persuasion*, 26.
2. Austen, *Persuasion*, 61.
3. Austen, *Persuasion*, 241.
4. Austen, *Persuasion*, 28.
5. Austen, *Persuasion*, 240.

## Day 21  Fervent in Prayer

1. Austen, *Mansfield Park*, 86.
2. Austen, *Mansfield Park*, 86.
3. Austen, *Mansfield Park*, 86.
4. Austen, *Mansfield Park*, 86.
5. Austen, *Mansfield Park*, 87.

## Day 22  Redeeming the Time

1. Austen, *Sense and Sensibility*, 5.
2. Austen, *Sense and Sensibility*, 5.
3. Austen, *Sense and Sensibility*, 8.
4. Austen, *Sense and Sensibility*, 13.

## Day 23  Make Us Like You

1. *Blue Letter Bible*, Strong's Definitions, s.v. "*forbearance*," www.blueletterbible.org /lang/lexicon/lexicon.cfm?Strongs=G463&t=KJV.

2. *Blue Letter Bible*, Strong's Definitions, s.v. "*patience*," www.blueletterbible.org/lang/lexicon/lexicon.cfm?Strongs=G3114&t=KJV.

3. Austen, *Pride and Prejudice*, 134.

4. Austen, *Pride and Prejudice*, 129.

5. Austen, *Pride and Prejudice*, 134.

## Day 24  Search Our Hearts, O God

1. Austen, *Mansfield Park*, 74.

2. Austen, *Mansfield Park*, 159.

## Day 25  Inexpressible Joy

1. Austen, *Letters*, 39.

2. Austen, *Letters*, 17.

3. Austen, *Letters*, 39.

## Day 26  Blessed Beyond Deserving

1. Austen, *Pride and Prejudice*, 43.

## Day 27  Morning Dawns and Evening Fades

1. Austen, *Letters*, 144.

## Day 28  Go into the World

1. Collins, *Parson's Daughter*, xviii.

2. Austen, *Mansfield Park*, 23.

3. Austen, *Mansfield Park*, 426.

4. Austen, *Mansfield Park*, 427.

5. Austen, *Mansfield Park*, 451.

6. Austen, *Mansfield Park*, 462.

7. Austen, *Mansfield Park*, 462.

8. Austen, *Mansfield Park*, 462.

## Day 29  Look with Compassion

1. Caroline Austen, *My Aunt Jane*, 11.

2. Austen, *My Aunt Jane*, 16–17.

3. Austen, *My Aunt Jane*, 17.

4. Austen, *Letters*, 360.

5. Austen, *Letters*, 360.
6. Austen, *Letters*, 361.
7. Austen, *Letters*, 361.
8. Austen, *Letters*, 363.

## Day 30  Thy Heavenly Kingdom

1. Austen, *My Aunt Jane*, 16.
2. Austen, *Letters*, 361.
3. Austen, *Letters*, 363.

## Day 31  Our Father

1. *The Book of Common Prayer*, 252.

## Epilogue  A Lasting Legacy

1. Austen, *Letters*, 359–60.
2. Paula Hollingsworth, *The Spirituality of Jane Austen* (Oxford: Lion Books, 2017), 164.
3. Hollingsworth, *The Spirituality of Jane Austen*, 165.
4. Austen-Leigh, *Memoir*, chap. 6.

# BIBLIOGRAPHY

Austen, Caroline. *My Aunt Jane: A Memoir (1867)*. Winchester, UK: Sarsen Press, 1952.

Austen, Jane. *Emma*. Edited by R. W. Chapman. Oxford: Oxford University Press, 1988.

Austen, Jane. *Jane Austen's Letters*. Edited by Deirdre Le Faye. 4th ed. Oxford: Oxford University Press, 2011.

Austen, Jane. *Mansfield Park*. Edited by R. W. Chapman. Oxford: Oxford University Press, 1988.

Austen, Jane. *Northanger Abbey*. Edited by R. W. Chapman. Oxford: Oxford University Press, 1988.

Austen, Jane. *Persuasion*. Edited by R. W. Chapman. Oxford: Oxford University Press, 1988.

Austen, Jane. *Pride and Prejudice*. Edited by R. W. Chapman. Oxford: Oxford University Press, 1988.

Austen, Jane. *Sense and Sensibility*. Edited by R. W. Chapman. Oxford: Oxford University Press, 1988.

Austen-Leigh, James Edward. *Memoir of Jane Austen (1870)*. CreateSpace Independent Publishing, 2014.

Austen-Leigh, William and Richard Arthur Austen-Leigh. *Jane Austen: Her Life and Letters (1913)*. New York: Barnes & Noble, 2006.

*The Book of Common Prayer: The Texts of 1549, 1559, and 1662.* Edited by Brian Cummings. Oxford: Oxford University Press, 2013.

Collins, Irene. *Jane Austen: The Parson's Daughter.* London: Bloomsbury, 1998.

Hill, Constance. *Jane Austen: Her Homes & Her Friends (1901).* Dodo Press, 2008.

Hollingsworth, Paula. *The Spirituality of Jane Austen.* Oxford: Lion Books, 2017.

Lane, Maggie. *Jane Austen's Family: Through Five Generations.* London: Robert Hale, 1984.

Le Faye, Deirdre. *Jane Austen: The World of Her Novels.* London: Frances Lincoln, 2002.

Stovel, Bruce. "'A Nation Improving in Religion': Jane Austen's Prayers and Their Place in Her Life and Art." *Persuasions*, no. 16 (1994): 185–196. www.jasna.org/persuasions/printed/number16/stovel.htm.

White, Laura Mooneyham. *Jane Austen's Anglicanism.* London: Routledge Taylor & Francis Group: 2011. Kindle.

# About the Author

Rachel Dodge teaches college English and Jane Austen classes, gives talks at libraries, teas, and Jane Austen groups, and is a writer for the popular *Jane Austen's World* blog. She is passionate about telling stories that bring God glory and about encouraging and equipping families to grow closer to Jesus through prayer and the study of God's Word. A true Janeite at heart, Rachel enjoys books, bonnets, and ball gowns. She makes her home in California with her husband and two children. Find out more at www.racheldodge.com.